T0318287

TEXTUAL PRACTICE

VOLUME 3

NUMBER 2

SUMMER 1989

Cambridge

Myth, Truth and Literature

Towards a True Post-Modernism
COLIN FALCK
This book is a theoretical study which aims to prove the superfluousness
of literary theory. Colin Falck argues that a 'paradigm-shift' is now
required which will replace 'structuralist' and 'post-structuralist' literary
theory and will re-establish the validity of such old-fashioned 'Romantic'
notions as intuition, inspiration and imagination.
£25.00 net   0 521 36256 3   204 pp.

Collected Essays

Volume 3: The Novel of Religious Controversy
Q. D. LEAVIS
Edited by **G. SINGH**
This third volume of Q. D. Leavis's essays brings together pieces on
hitherto unexplored aspects of Victorian literature. Most of these are
previously unpublished and there are essays and reviews which originally
appeared in *Scrutiny*. Mrs Leavis approaches her subject from a literary-
historical and sociological point of view.
£30.00 net   0 521 26703 X   356 pp.

Shakespeare Survey 41

Shakespearian Stages and Staging (with an index to *Surveys 31-40*)
Edited by **STANLEY WELLS**
This latest edition of the *Shakespeare Survey* examines the staging of
many of the plays or individual scenes, from contemporary productions
to the present. It also looks at performances in London and Stratford in
1986-7.
£30.00 net   0 521 36071 4   320 pp.

The Origins of Modern Critical Thought

German Aesthetic and Literary Criticism from Lessing to Hegel
Edited by **DAVID SIMPSON**
This is the most comprehensive anthology in English of the major texts
of German literary and aesthetic theory between Lessing and Hegel. The
texts are crucial not only to the Romantic period itself, but also as the
source of modern literary theory.
£30.00 net   Hc   0 521 35004 2   458 pp.
£10.95 net   Pb   0 521 35902 3

Cambridge
University Press

The Edinburgh Building, Cambridge CB2 2RU

TEXTUAL PRACTICE

Editor

Textual Practice will be published three times a year, in spring, summer and winter, by Routledge Journals, 11 New Fetter Lane, London, EC4P 4EE. All rights are reserved. No part of the publication may be reprinted, reproduced or utilized in any form or by any electronic, mechanical, or other means, now known or hearafter invented, including photocopying and recording, or in any information storage or retrieval system, without permission in writing from the author(s) and publishers, but academic institutions may make not more than three xerox copies of any one article in any single issue without needing further permission; all enquiries to the Editor.

Contributions and correspondence should be addressed to the Editor at University of Wales College of Cardiff.

Books for review and related correspondence should be addressed to Christopher Norris at the School of English Studies, Journalism and Philosophy, University of Wales College of Cardiff, PO Box 94, Cardiff CF1 3XE.

Advertisements Enquiries to David Polley, Routledge Journals, 11 New Fetter Lane, London EC4P 4EE.

Subscription rates (calendar year only: UK full: £38.50; UK personal £24.00; Rest of World full: £40.00; Rest of World personal: £26.00; USA full: $72.00; USA personal: $48.00. All rates include postage; airmail rates on application. Subscriptions to: Subscriptions Department, Routledge Journals, North Way, Andover, Hants, SP10 5BE.

ISSN 0950-236X
Typeset by Columns, Reading

© Routledge 1989

Transferred to Digital Printing 2004

Contents

CATHERINE BELSEY
Towards cultural history – in theory and practice

I

Is there a place for English in a postmodern world? Does an academy where twentieth-century textual practice breaks down the nineteenth-century boundaries between disciplines offer English departments any worthwhile job to do? Can we still seriously set out to teach our students literature?

I start from the assumption that English as it has traditionally been understood, as the study of great literary works by great authors, has no useful part to play in a pedagogy committed to a politics of change. In the course of the 1980s the institution of English has been firmly stripped of its mask of polite neutrality by Peter Widdowson, Chris Baldick, Terry Eagleton and Terence Hawkes, among others.[1] As their analyses reveal, the conservatism of traditional English lies primarily in two main areas: first, its promotion of the author-subject as the individual origin of meaning, insight, and truth; and second, its claim that this truth is universal, transcultural and ahistorical. In this way, English affirms as natural and inevitable both the individualism and the world picture of a specific western culture, and within that culture the perspective of a specific class and a specific sex. In other words, a discipline that purports to be outside politics in practice reproduces a very specific political position.

But I start equally from the assumption that there is no special political or pedagogical merit in severing all ties with the texts the institution of English has done its best to make its own. It would be ironic if a theory of difference left us unable to differentiate between Bradley's *Othello* and Leavis's, and between these *Othellos* and all the others we might produce for quite other purposes. It would be still more ironic if by a kind of political ultra-leftism we abandoned *Othello* and the entire institution – with all its (precisely institutional) power – and handed it back without a struggle to those for whom a politics of change is more of a threat than a promise. The works that the institution of English has done everything to appropriate are there to be reclaimed and reappropriated, and there is no reason why this should not be done from within the institution. The texts are available to be reread as the material for a history of meanings and values and practices in their radical discontinuity. In this way new work might be expected to come from the English department itself, and not just from somewhere else called, say, Cultural Studies. My project for English, therefore, is not to abandon it but to *move* it – towards cultural history.

Much of the work of the institution has been, of course, a process of exclusion. The canon of great books by great authors has been important not only for what it affirms – the value and the coherence of admissible readings of those works it recognizes. As every feminist, for example, knows, its importance also lies in what it refuses. Dale Spender has recently unearthed nearly 600 novels from the century before Jane Austen, by a hundred women novelists who were taken seriously in their own period. As she points out, Ian Watt's extremely influential book, *The Rise of the Novel*, takes no account of their existence. As far as the institution is concerned, the novel was invented by men. *The Rise of the Novel* is subtitled *Studies in Defoe, Richardson and Fielding*.[2]

The relegation of certain authors, of particular texts and, above all, of specific textual practices helps to police the boundaries of truth. Texts which are most obviously difficult to recuperate, which most obviously challenge conservative assumptions about race, class, or gender, have been systematically marginalized as 'flawed', or banished from view (and in consequence from print) as inadequate, not *literature*. They are, of course, flawed and inadequate according to literary standards invoked precisely to marginalize them – standards which have denied their own relativity, and indeed the cultural and historical specificity of imposing 'literary standards' at all.

The cultural history I should like to see us produce would refuse nothing. While of course any specific investigation would find a specific focus, both chronologically and textually, no moment, no epoch, no genre and no form of signifying practice would be excluded a priori from the field of enquiry. Cultural history would have no place for a canon, and no interest in ranking works in order of merit. Stephen Greenblatt's discussion of the reformer Tyndale, for instance, in his book *Renaissance Self-Fashioning*, shows some of the advantages of linking literature with a manual of religious politics in the analysis of sixteenth-century subjectivity. Greenblatt treats *The Obedience of a Christian Man* not as background in the conventional way, but as text.[3] Indeed, Louis Adrian Montrose, like Greenblatt an American New Historicist, identifies his own position in terms which closely resemble the project I am trying to define here. New Historicism is new, Montrose points out, 'in its refusal of traditional distinctions between literature and history, between text and context; new in resisting a traditional opposition of the privileged individual – whether an author or a work – to a world "outside" '.[4] In a rather different way, Jacqueline Rose's book on *Peter Pan* also rejects traditional distinctions and oppositions. Rose brings together children's fiction, the notion of the child and the history of sexuality in ways that throw into relief the limitations on our knowledge imposed by conventional value-judgments and conventional reading practices.[5] Without wanting to deny the specificity of fiction, of genre and, indeed, of the individual text, cultural history would necessarily take all signifying practice as its domain.

And that means that the remaining demarcation lines between disciplines would not survive the move. Signifying practice is not exclusively nor even primarily verbal. We need, for example, to align ourselves with art historians. I have invoked portraits in the analysis of changing meanings of gender relations.[6] John Barrell and Norman Bryson have both in different ways demonstrated much more extensively the kind of work that becomes possible when writing and painting are brought into conjunction, without treating one as the background which explains the other.[7] And perhaps more eccentrically, but only marginally so, the allocation of domestic space is replete with meanings for the cultural historian. The medieval move of the feast from the hall to the great chamber, which was also for sleeping in (or rather, to the great chambers, since the lady, if she was involved in the feast at all, was likely to dine in her own chamber),[8] and the subsequent isolation of the family dining-room from the servants' quarters, is as significant in charting the history of the meaning of the family as is the current vogue for open-plan living. What is at stake in each of these changes is the definition of the family unit. And meanwhile, Girouard's account of the development of the privy in his book on the English country house constitutes a mine of information indispensable to any truly thorough analysis of the bourgeois disavowal of the body.[9]

II

As this rudimentary reading list reveals, I don't imagine that cultural history is my own invention. It is necessary only to point to the work of Christopher Hill and E. P. Thompson, or of Philippe Ariès and Marina Warner, to give authority to such a project. Here fiction is one source, and not necessarily a privileged one, of knowledge about the past. Meanwhile, the recent phase of feminist criticism received a considerable impetus from three books published in 1970 by Kate Millett, Germaine Greer, and Eva Figes. All three discussed literature, and all three refused to isolate it from the culture of which it formed a part. The writings of Freud and Barbara Cartland, for example, were invoked by these feminists, and were treated neither as explanatory metalanguage in the first case, nor as cultural context in the second, but in both instances as texts alongside Shakespeare, D. H. Lawrence, and Norman Mailer. And, of course, the transformation of English into cultural history would be unthinkable without the example of Raymond Williams, who above all established a tradition of radical critical work from within the institution of English itself.

But in listing this methodologically and politically disparate group of writers, I become conscious of the need at this stage to clarify precisely what it is that cultural history enables us to know, and to reflect on why it is that we might want to know it. Without intending at all to diminish the radical importance of their work, or my own debts to all of them, I am not now sure that every form of knowledge that each of these authors has pursued is either available to us on the one hand or politically productive on the other.

Early in *Of Grammatology*, Derrida, whose admirers have so often presented him as contemptuous of history, suggests that there remains to be written a history of writing itself, or rather, a history of what he calls 'the system of signified truth'.[10] What Derrida is proposing here is the story of God, of the transcendental signified which holds all other meanings in place, and he offers a series of quotations from different historical moments which identify the truth as alternatively God or his surrogates, nature, reason, the self. (Derrida is explicitly discussing a continuity here, but he of all people would hardly be likely to rule out some very significant differences between these terms.) And early in volume 2 of *The History of Sexuality* Foucault, whose admirers are so often anxious to see his work in opposition to Derrida's, gives a general account of his own project: 'what I have held to, what I have tried to maintain for many years, is the effort to isolate some of the elements that might be useful for a history of truth'.[11] For all their important differences, Derrida and Foucault both identify a mode of history which is profoundly political. To possess the truth is to have the right to act in its name. Truth stands outside culture as a guarantee of legitimacy. Despite the familiar romance of truth, secretly so dear to academics, in which the special and solitary hero sets out to go beyond the bounds of convention on a lonely quest for transcendental presence, in historical practice the metaphysics of truth has licensed torture, exploitation, and mass murder. Poststructuralism now displays truth as a linguistic tyranny which arrests the proliferation of meanings, assigns values and specifies norms. Truth recruits subjects. The history of truth is the history of our subjection. Its content is the knowledges that constitute us as subjects, and that define and delimit what it is possible for us to say, to be and to do.

It might be worth a digression here to stress the argument that to abandon truth is not necessarily to embrace the free-for-all of radical subjectivism. And it is not inevitably to endorse a politics of relativism or, worse, expediency. The proposition is that we cannot *know* that any existing language maps the world adequately, that there can be no certainty of a fit between the symbolic and the real. This is not the same as encouraging people to subscribe to whatever conviction happens to come into their heads, or inciting them to make things up. Nor is it to settle for believing them when they do. It is perfectly possible to recognize lies without entailing the possibility of telling the truth, least of all the whole truth. It would be very naïve indeed to claim that people do not from time to time set out to deceive each other, or that institutions and states do not practise cover-ups on a deplorable scale. But what they conceal is what they know, and since there can be no guarantee that any system of differences maps the world accurately, knowledge is necessarily culturally and discursively relative. This does not exonerate the liars. They are culpable. But neither does it support the belief that in order to be able to denounce lies, we have to cling to a metaphysics of truth. Language is a system of differences, not of binary oppositions. As Foucault argues in another but related context, alternatives which only offer either the old constraints or no constraints at all are 'simplistic and authoritarian', and we should refuse to be coerced by them.[12] You can tell it like you know it, in accordance with the rules of the discourse, without having to claim that you're telling it like it (absolutely, metaphysically, incontrovertibly) *is*.

It is my empirical observation, offered here for debate, that whereas men in general have the greatest difficulty in surrendering the concept of truth, women in general do so without much trouble. The explanation is almost certainly not biological. The cultural construction of women – as of other marginal groups – tends to include rather less emphasis on the possession of truth. Marginal subjects commonly have an oblique relationship to the world map which guarantees the imaginary knowing, mastering autonomy of those who speak from the centre of a culture. The map always represents a knowledge of which those at the margins are at least partly the objects rather than the subjects, and from which they are at least from time to time excluded. Their identity as subjects is thus less evidently dependent on the reaffirmation of the map itself. Conversely, however, marginality of this kind protects women from the fear that if the world is not exactly as we have mapped it, perhaps it is not there at all, or the conviction that the alternative to truth is chaos or absence. As women, we know that, whatever form it may take, the real is there and is independent of our will: we are, after all, consistently assaulted, constrained, defined and reconstructed by it. Cartesian doubt, Catharine MacKinnon points out, 'comes from the luxury of a position of power that entails the possibility of making the world as one thinks it to be'.[13] Most women, however individually powerful, have only a sporadic or oblique hold on that luxury; they can therefore relinquish the totalizing narratives of their culture with relative equanimity.

III

If the ultimate objective of a politically radical cultural history is the history of truth, its location is the history of meanings. Not exactly concerned with images and representations, in so far as those terms indicate an exteriority, gesture towards a presence which is always elsewhere, cultural history is nevertheless not quite a history of behaviour or conduct either. The project is to identify the meanings in circulation in earlier periods, to specify the discourses, conventions and signifying practices by which meanings are fixed, norms 'agreed' and truth defined. Cultural history is thus a history of 'experience' only, as Foucault puts it, 'where experience is understood as the correlation between fields of knowledge, types of normativity, and forms of subjectivity in a particular culture'.[14] The constraints on knowledge, normativity, and subjectivity are the ranges of meaning culturally and discursively available. What it is possible to 'experience' at any specific moment is an effect of what it is possible to say. (Not, of course, what I am personally capable of formulating, but *what can be said* and thus known.) And in case this proposition should be interpreted as a piece of unregenerate structuralism, it is perhaps useful to reaffirm that meanings are always plural, subject to excess, in process, contradictory, sites of struggle.

It is important to bear in mind, too, that wherever there is a history of subjection to norms and truths, there is also a history of resistances. Power produces resistance not only as its legitimation, as the basis for an extension of control, but as its defining difference, the other which endows it with meaning, visibility, effectivity. The work of Foucault is an important influence here. His position is often represented, by Foucault's admirers and his detractors alike, as negative, nihilistic, an account of power as a new transcendental signified, irreducible and irresistible in its omnipresence. Some of the New Historicists have borrowed from Foucault in order to produce an account of history, especially Renaissance history, which is so close in many ways to the kind of cultural history I am proposing here that it seems important to attempt to distinguish between the two. Of course, New Historicism is by no means a unified phenomenon, and any generalization is likely to obliterate important differences of emphasis. But if it is possible to point to general tendencies, this is a form of cultural history in which power is commonly seen as centred, usually in the monarchy, and is held to produce opposition only in order to legitimate its own extension. In practice, this analysis owes more to functionalism than it does to Foucault, who locates power not in a centre, but in knowledges, discourses, micro-exchanges, and who everywhere proclaims its precariousness, its instability. On the assumption that political usefulness, not the author's opinion, is our concern, Foucault's work can be read, selectively, I admit, but no less productively for that, as a history of resistances – of ballad-mongers, fools, criminals, deviants and suicides who heroically repudiate the positions that power produces for them.

If there is a general distinction to be made between the project of the New Historicists and what I am proposing here, it lies in the inscription of struggle. Too often in the work of Stephen Greenblatt and Jonathan Goldberg, for all its elegance, scholarship, and subtlety, power is represented as seamless and all-pervasive, while resistance, where it exists at all, is seen as ultimately self-deceived. Texts are understood as homogeneous, monologic, in the last instance non-contradictory, because the uncertainties they formulate are finally contained by the power they might seem to subvert.[15] The cultural history I propose is a story of conflicting interests, of heroic refusals, of textual uncertainties. It tells of power, but of power which always entails the possibility of resistance, in so far as it inevitably requires a differentiating other.

To this extent, then, I share the position of the British Cultural

Materialists, who tend to stress subversion rather than containment. But in this case too it seems to me important to draw distinctions between an existing practice and the project I am outlining.[16] It is even less clear here than in the case of New Historicism that there is a single, homogeneous body of work to which the term Cultural Materialism refers. The phrase was originally invoked by Raymond Williams, and was subsequently adopted by Jonathan Dollimore and Alan Sinfield as the subtitle of their important and challenging collection of essays on *Political Shakespeare*.[17] It seems to imply an allusion to the Althusserian concept of ideology as a material practice, and to propose that culture, like Althusser's ideology, is relatively autonomous and is in consequence itself a site of contradiction and struggle. The structuralist analysis of the materiality of language had made it possible for Althusser to break with a vulgarized Marxist treatment of ideology as the *expression* of a struggle which was *really* taking place elsewhere, in the economy. Now the economic, the political, and the ideological could be thought as distinct instances, relatively independent, developing unevenly, but linked together to the extent that each might also constitute a condition of the possibility of developments in the others. Althusser's term 'ideology', however, though indispensable in enabling theory to break with the empiricist recuperation of Marx, has come in time to seem rather a blunt instrument, if only because of the uneasy distinction in Althusser's own writing between *ideologies* and *ideology in general.* (It was at this point that Foucault's work on the power relations inscribed in knowledges-as-discourses offered the possibility of a more focused analysis of cultural practice.) In the usage of Dollimore and Sinfield the looser term, 'culture', in conjunction with the silent allusion to Marxism in the word 'materialism', appears to promise a form of analysis which takes into account post-Althusserian work on the textual inscription of struggle.

It is disappointing, therefore, to find that in Dollimore's introduction to *Political Shakespeare* the emphasis is on cultural subversion as a unitary phenomenon, as an 'idea', which is 'represented' (re-presented) in texts, and that the real struggle is once again elsewhere:

> the mere thinking of a radical idea is not what makes it subversive . . . one might go further and suggest that not only does the idea have to be conveyed, it has also actually to be used to refuse authority *or* be seen by authority as capable and likely of being so used.

'Ideas' apparently have materiality only if they are in some not very clearly specified way *put into* practice, or *perceived as* able to be so. Later in the same paragraph an idea is subversive because it is 'taken up' and helps to precipitate 'historical change'.[18] There is no space in Dollimore's account of Cultural Materialism for the theoretical developments of recent years, for the analysis of textuality as inherently unstable, or for the identification of culture as itself the place where norms are specified and contested, knowledges affirmed and challenged, and subjectivity produced and disrupted.

If meanings are not fixed and guaranteed, but as Derrida has consistently argued, indeterminate, differed and deferred, invaded by the trace of otherness which defines and constitutes the self-same, texts necessarily exceed their own unitary projects, whether these are subversion or containment, in a movement of instability which releases new possibilities in the very process of attempting to close them off. And if power generates the possibility of resistance as its defining difference, the signified truth necessarily produces alternative knowledges, not only for political motives, as functionalism proposes, in order to master them, but also as a structural necessity, because without them it lacks definition. Only an eternal verity (universal truth) can hold the network of meanings in place. But it does so in a perpetual conflict with its others, both internal and external, which is the condition of its existence as knowledge. If we succeed in relativizing the truth, then we release as material for analysis the play of signification, Foucault's 'games of truth',[19] which necessarily have more than one player, or more than one side, and which are not a reflection of the struggle for power, but its location. To give a historical account of what constitutes us as subjects is to specify the possibilities of transgressing the existing limits on what we are able to say, to be and to do.[20]

IV

What has this to do with the institution of English? Everything, I believe. More than any other discipline, English has been concerned with the study of signifying practice. Traditionally we have not only analysed meanings (philosophy does that too), and we have not only been concerned with social relations (history and sociology are too). Supremely, English departments have attended to the formal properties of texts, their modes of address to readers and the conditions in which they are intelligible. Cultural history needs to appropriate and develop those strategies, putting them to work not in order to demonstrate the value of the text, or its coherence as the expression of the authorial subjectivity which is its origin, but to lay bare the contradictions and conflicts, the instabilities and indeterminacies, which inevitably reside in any bid for truth. We need only extend the range of texts we are willing to discuss, to put on the syllabus . . .

That 'only' is there to cheer us up, to make it all sound easy. I'm not sure how easy it is. But if we can interpret Shakespeare, we can surely learn to interpret fashion, and music – and privies. Fredric Jameson has succeeded with an ease which may be deceptive (or which at least may be hard to emulate) in bringing together fiction, painting, music, film, and architecture in his polemical and controversial account of the postmodern condition.

Jameson's essay, 'Postmodernism, or the cultural logic of late capitalism', is a discussion of changes in signifying practice itself: not simply changes in meaning in the conventional sense, but changes in form.[21] It is impossible to consider postmodernism without paying attention to its mode of address, its disruption of the subject-object couple produced and reproduced by the signifying practices of classic realism. What Jameson fears – and others celebrate – is the dispersal of the knowing subject of humanism, in possession of the objects of its knowledge, and able to map the world. In my book *The Subject of Tragedy* I suggested that the subject of humanism was installed as a consequence of a parallel shift in signifying practice in the sixteenth and seventeenth centuries. My aim there was not to declare a nostalgia for the world we have lost, but to chart a revolution in the system of signification, which had radical implications for the subjectivity that is its effect. There is a great deal more work to be done on the specificity of modes of address and the history of the subject. And if this particular task seems to me especially urgent, that is perhaps because our culture places the subject at the centre of the system of signified truths, identifies it as the absolute, extra-linguistic presence which is the origin and guarantee of the fixity of meaning, and targets nuclear weapons on the Soviet Union in defence of its (imaginary) freedom. If in the twentieth century truth has at last become plural, it is still inclined to be subjective, the unique and inalienable property of each unique individual subject.

Or it was. Because the tyranny of truth (including the subjective truth) becomes visible to us now only in consequence of the postmodern condition. It is no accident, but a precise effect of cultural history, that postmodern practice and poststructuralist theory coincide in their assault on truth to the extent that they do.

This is not to say that our own position as individuals – for or against truth, theory, change – is determined for us in advance: that too is a site of struggle, of subjections and resistances. There are choices constantly to be made, but they are political choices, choices of subject-position, not recognitions of the truth. It is, however, to emphasize our location within a continuing history, and the relativity of our own meanings, knowledges and practices. And perhaps this above all is the pedagogic and political importance of cultural history. It addresses and constitutes students, readers, practitioners who are themselves an effect of the history they make.

It goes without saying (I hope) after all this that I am not proposing that we should set out in quest of a new truth, simply reconstituting our dispersed, postmodern subjectivities round new objects of knowledge. Still less that we reconstruct the institution of English in support of a more comprehensive metanarrative, a more thorough mapping of the world, a new system centred on a new transcendental signified. Nor on the other hand is cultural relativity the ground of a simple libertarianism, making the texts do whatever we like. This part of my argument is difficult to formulate, since the discourse of a non-empiricist knowledge barely exists as yet, but I am persuaded that we should not abandon the notion of rigour, the project of substantiating our readings, or a commitment to historical specificity. We shall need principles of selection, since without them no individual project would be thinkable. But at the same time, the cultural history I visualize is predicated on the relativity of knowledges, on history as a process of production, and on that process as political intervention.

If, however, it takes for granted the relativity of our certainties, it also assumes the relativity of our subjection. The transcendental subject, outside and above the objects of its knowledge, is also the most deeply subjected being, at the mercy of the system of signified truth of which it is an effect. Conversely, the subjectivity which is imbricated in the knowledges it participates in and helps to produce has more options at its disposal. Modes of resistance – or, to use Pêcheux's terms, counter identification, the rejection of what is dominant, and disidentification, the production of alternative knowledges, alternative subject positions – are no longer seen as eccentric or psychotic, as a threat to the very being of the subject itself. A subjectivity explicitly constituted in and by its own knowledges does not 'disintegrate' in consequence of contradiction and conflict. And equally, it escapes to some degree the reaffirmation of the lack which stems from the exteriority of a knowledge whose objects are always finally elsewhere, beyond the grasp of the subject. The readings we should make would not be a quest for lost presence, but a contribution to a continuing process of production.

The project, then, is a history of meanings, and struggles for meaning, in every place where meanings can be found – or made. Its focus is on change, cultural difference and the relativity of truth. And its purpose is to change the subject, involving ourselves as practitioners in the political and pedagogic process of making history, in both senses of that phrase.

V

This proposal, though largely theoretical, is not in fact wholly abstract. In the autumn of 1986, as Visiting Professor at McMaster University, Hamilton, Ontario, I had the opportunity to teach a graduate class on a topic of my choice. I chose 'Towards Cultural History' as my title, and devised a course which I hoped would enable me to see how the theory I have outlined might work in practice. The students were excellent: they were co-operative, diligent, adventurous, enthusiastic and intelligent. They cannot be held in any way responsible for the fact that the course ran into certain difficulties – and that these difficulties represent problems I am still not sure how to solve.

In order to define the problems, it is necessary to give a brief account of what we did. Since my appointment was only for one term, we had a total of thirteen weeks. Some of the students were entirely new to poststructuralist theory, though some had a very sophisticated grasp of recent theoretical debates. It seemed to me imperative that the class should arrive at some sort of consensus on what it was possible to know. The alternative, the danger of having to be present at or take part in metaphysical discussions about the inaccessible intentions of specific authors, or the ineffable experience of particular groups of people, seemed to me – and still seems – extremely dispiriting. We therefore set out on the one hand to engage with the basic theories of language, subjectivity and knowledge which have produced poststructuralism, but on the other to alternate our attention to theory with the practice of cultural history.

In accordance with this plan, I offered at our first meeting an example of the kind of cultural history I proposed, an analysis of Holbein's *The Ambassadors* in conjunction with a scene from *Hamlet*, and a discussion of the relations between humanism, illusionism and violence. Thereafter there were no more set pieces from me. In each class we discussed the week's required reading on the basis of brief papers produced by individual students.

We had a good time. We had a particularly good time with the theory. We struggled with and over passages of Derrida, Althusser, and Foucault. We agreed to read *The Use of Pleasure*, the second volume of Foucault's *History of Sexuality*. This was still in hardback and a major expense for the students, but we were determined to be up-to-date. We discussed it and pooled our disappointment. Where, we wondered, was the evidence of resistance here? Where was the symptomatic textual analysis which would betray as precarious, as unstable, the regimes of self-discipline the book was concerned to analyse? We all wanted to get the theory straight: we all wanted to debate its value; we all wanted to discuss its political implications. We found that we agreed to a surprising extent, though there was enough scepticism in the group to keep us going.

But we had trouble with the practice, with the production of our own contribution to cultural history. The first time we tried to put the theory into practice, I showed slides of family portraits from different periods. We 'read' them together, and identified in the visual images the changing inscription of patriarchal and proprietary power relations. We produced some impressive interpretations and distinctions, but it all seemed a little bit facile – perhaps because we didn't know enough to relate our readings to contemporary cultural phenomena from a range of distinct historical moments. In consequence, we were not convinced that we had been able to produce an account of the meanings of the family which was sufficiently detailed and sufficiently nuanced to be satisfying. At other times the students produced analyses they had worked on. The rest of us were willing to be impressed, but we didn't necessarily feel we knew enough to comment critically or to contribute by drawing new inferences.

It would have defeated the object of the exercise, however, if I had simply provided the materials for the students to reaffirm instances of cultural history which I had already produced (or at least defined) ahead of them. The project was not that the students should master an existing map of cultural history, but that they should contribute to a future one. But this presents serious theoretical and pedagogical problems. As English is traditionally taught, the map is drawn for the students in advance (and in some cases a very long time in advance: individual syllabuses have been known to last for thirty years, and the present literary canon in its broad outlines has been there longer still). Even in the relatively rare instances where the course includes material that has not been taught before – women's writing, black writing or postmodern fiction, for example – the texts tend to be specified ahead of time. The same goes for the theoretical element of the cultural history course: the classic texts of poststructuralism are reasonably well established (though by no means beyond dispute, of course). But how, without pre-empting the production process itself, was it possible to structure a seminar which could do the practical work? The production of cultural history was not a problem in itself. But the question was how to integrate the production process into a course, how to involve other people in the work, how to share the practice in the way that we shared the discussion of the theory.

That definition of the problem points at once to the solution. If we had had another term for the course, I think we ought to have spent it devising and realizing the collective production of a specific piece of cultural history. Mercifully, perhaps, in view of the real difficulties of collective work in the deeply individualist culture of the free west, especially within the profoundly un-collective framework of North American tertiary education, there wasn't time. But if there had been, could we have done it?

There would have been serious institutional problems. How could we have negotiated the students' very real need for individual grades? And what would my position have been? A disinterested observer? An equal member of the collective? And if the second of these, what would have happened when I suddenly took up a quite different position as assessor, allotting grades on behalf of the institution? Would there have been time within the constraints of a course to discuss the solutions to these problems collectively, to choose a project collectively, and also to produce something worthwhile at the end of it all? And if we had failed to produce a worthwhile piece of cultural history, would that have invalidated the whole project, leaving us all in despair?

Some of these problems are already familiar from the debates of the 1960s (which in practice were largely the 1970s, as far as more British universities were concerned). But the problems then were not exactly the same as they are now. At that time the issues were primarily 'relevance' and a new (and probably very necessary) libertarianism. The most prominent pedagogic question was how to allow students to exercise greater choice about their areas of study and greater control over their mode of work. It is worth saying that we did not entirely solve those problems. But the new issue, foregrounded by postmodernism in its distrust of metanarratives, fixed knowledges, maps, is how to avoid charting the terrain in advance, merely asking students to traverse existing and well-worn paths to known destinations.

A number of these difficulties would disappear, or at least dwindle, in an institution widely committed to the practice of cultural history. A single course in isolation has to cover all the ground; it must be sure to include both theory and practice; and it operates under pressure to offer a model of what cultural history might be. For all these reasons it has some responsibility not simply to pursue the current interests of the teacher concerned. But a whole graduate programme in cultural history, complete with a separate theory course and a range of options, could afford to do precisely that. In those circumstances, where plurality was built in from the beginning, we could afford to involve our students in our own current projects, working out jointly with them a plan of work and a mode of analysis.

Although in these circumstances some of the institutional problems would remain, the scheme of study I have outlined could, I believe, be put into practice. The educational institution as it already exists produces alternative knowledges as its difference, so that we can all as individuals 'do' cultural history if we choose. It should not, therefore, prove impossible to devise and implement a pedagogy that permits us to introduce courses in cultural history as a genuinely radical alternative to the simultaneous individualism and universalism of English in its traditional form.

It is for that reason that I have called this essay 'Towards cultural history'. It proposes a specific kind of journey, but it does not yet lay claim to an arrival.

University of Wales, Cardiff

NOTES

1 Peter Widdowson (ed.), *Re-Reading English* (London: Methuen, 1982); Chris Baldick, *The Social Mission of English Criticism, 1848–1932* (Oxford: Oxford University Press, 1983); Terry Eagleton, *Literary Theory: an Introduction* (Oxford: Basil Blackwell, 1983); Terence Hawkes, *That Shakespeherian Rag* (London: Methuen, 1986).
2 See Dale Spender, *Mothers of the Novel* (London: Pandora, 1986), pp. 115–37.
3 Stephen Greenblatt, *Renaissance Self-fashioning from More to Shakespeare* (Chicago: University of Chicago Press, 1980).
4 Louis Adrian Montrose, 'The Elizabethan subject and the Spenserian text', in Patricia Parker and David Quint (eds), *Literary Theory/Renaissance Texts* (Baltimore: Johns Hopkins University Press, 1986), pp. 303–40, 304.
5 Jacqueline Rose, *Peter Pan, or the Impossibility of Children's Fiction* (London: Macmillan, 1984).
6 Catherine Belsey, 'Disrupting sexual difference: meaning and gender in the comedies', in John Drakakis (ed.), *Alternative Shakespeares* (London: Methuen, 1985), pp. 166–90; *The Subject of Tragedy: Identity and Difference in Renaissance Drama* (London: Methuen, 1985).
7 John Barrell, *The Dark Side of the Landscape: the Rural Poor in English Painting 1730–1840* (Cambridge: Cambridge University Press, 1980); Norman Bryson, *Word and Image: French Painting of the Ancien Regime* (Cambridge: Cambridge University Press, 1981).

8 Mark Girouard, *Life in the English Country House* (Harmondsworth: Penguin Books, 1980).

9 ibid., pp. 245–66.

10 Jacques Derrida, *Of Grammatology*, tr. Gayatri Chakravorty Spivak (Baltimore: Johns Hopkins University Press, 1976), p. 15.

11 Michel Foucault, *The Use of Pleasure* (*The History of Sexuality*, vol. 2) (London: Viking Press, 1986), p. 6.

12 Michel Foucault, 'What is enlightenment?', in Paul Rabinow (ed.), *The Foucault Reader* (Harmondsworth: Penguin Books, 1986), pp. 32–50, 43.

13 Catharine A. MacKinnon, 'Desire and power: a feminist perspective', in Cary Nelson and Lawrence Grossberg (eds), *Marxism and the Interpretation of Culture* (London: Macmillan, 1988), pp. 105–21, 113.

14 Foucault, *The Use of Pleasure*, p. 4.

15 See Greenblatt, *Renaissance Self-fashioning*; Jonathan Goldberg, *James I and the Politics of Literature* (Baltimore: Johns Hopkins University Press, 1983). But for exceptions to these generalizations, see Louis Adrian Montrose, ' "Shaping fantasies": figurations of gender and power in Elizabethan culture', *Representations*, 1, 2 (Spring 1983), pp. 61–94; and 'The Elizabethan subject and the Spenserian text'.

16 On a visit to the United States in 1988 I was surprised to discover that I was a Cultural Materialist.

17 Jonathan Dollimore and Alan Sinfield (eds), *Political Shakespeare: New Essays in Cultural Materialism* (Manchester: Manchester University Press, 1985).

18 ibid., p. 13.

19 Foucault, *The Use of Pleasure*, pp. 6–7.

20 Foucault, 'What is enlightenment?', p. 46.

21 Fredric Jameson, 'Postmodernism, or the cultural logic of late capitalism', *New Left Review*, 146 (1984), pp. 53–92.

PAUL CARTER and DAVID MALOUF
Spatial History

(A transcript of a broadcast conversation between Paul Carter, author of *The Road to Botany Bay* (London: Faber & Faber, 1987; New York: Knopf, 1988) and the novelist David Malouf.)[1]

DM: I suppose it's proper, Paul, that you should find yourself talking to a writer rather than a professional historian or a geographer because, finally, what your book's about is the act of writing, isn't it?

PC: That's right. I'm interested in how writing itself is the medium of history. Writing isn't something that simply comments on events that occurred elsewhere. What we have – the original documents, maps, journals – are themselves sorts of writing, and I am interested in the relationship between the act of writing history and the original historical writings on which that process is based. It's likely that a book of this kind, which speculates about history *as writing*, is going to raise problems for a certain kind of historian, but perhaps be more immediately appealing to writers.

DM: But it goes beyond that, doesn't it, because you are saying that the medium through which we finally understand things and make them available to ourselves as areas of action is language itself – the articulating of spaces is what allows us to move.

PC: Quite early on in the book there's a long discussion in various contexts of the process of naming. Why did explorers name places? What I am saying there is that the act of naming didn't come *after* a place was found: it was actually through the act of naming that a space was delineated as having a character, something that could be referred to. A very important part of the language act was the creation of a space where one could move on to somewhere else. It was not that there was a stage, an already existing place where events could unfold in time – the significant early events in the European occupation of Australia have to do with creating an 'Australia', a named network through which, and in terms of which, certain historical events might begin to occur.

DM: That's made a difficulty for some readers, hasn't it? I mean, most books about history assume that Australia is there. There is a space in which you arrive and come ashore. You clear a bit of it and *then* something happens. The coming ashore is an act, the clearing is an act, but *only* then does history begin to happen. You really want to go way back beyond that and say: no, there are no pre-existing spaces, no pre-existing stages; what we have to do is make the space itself.

Part of your book is about how people make the spaces – they are made partly by your travelling in to them, partly by your describing them. That's what you mean by 'spatial history', isn't it? You go back beyond the original actions to ask yourself where these actions are *going to take place*, not where can they take place – and that's something quite radical in the real meaning of that word.

PC: As you say, there's been some difficulty in understanding what I mean by 'spatial history'. Interestingly, no one has commented on the illustrations in the book. A fair number of those illustrations are to do with incomplete maps. These remind us that Australia was not a fully charted outline. They show us individual journeys which peter out; they show us words like 'Nothing seen beyond this rise' or 'Dense brush in this direction'. Those statements are written *on the map* – the maps are not atlas maps yet, they are incomplete records of uncompleted journeys. They have to do with the way language is still being written over the imaginary space of the map. They are provisional.

In other words, the maps are obvious documents relating to the pre-history of the country. As yet there are places on those maps which are unnamed, unoccupied and, therefore, where nothing can happen, historically speaking.

DM: Unoccupied and unnamed by Europeans.

PC: Quite. As the book goes on to develop the argument, it's clear they are fully named, fully occupied and have their own spatial history – which is clearly the history given to them by the Aborigines.

So the maps are one way of evoking Australia's spatial history. But there's another aspect to the process.

When one starts talking about writing 'an *essay* in spatial history', you are obliged, I think, to consider the shape of the narrative itself. If we're going to say that before we can have history as a plot with characters we have got to map out the terrain where this is to occur, then you have to think about the shape of the book itself. It can't be a narrative history, nor can it be a history with a set of definitions. Definitions are like capital cities – we haven't got any in this landscape yet.

So the book was written as a set of provisional stopping points and, to ensure that the journey didn't peter out, the spatial history was 'essayed' in the form of a journey out and a journey back. Hence we have a reflection on certain themes emerging in the first half occurring in the second half – the picturesque, first discussed in Chapter 4, is discussed from a quite different point of view in Chapter 8, in the second half of the book.

As an essay in this new topic of spatial history, it seemed to me essential to embody the notion I wanted to express in the writing. Of course, for people wanting quick definitions, it was hard to find the definitive point of arrival. But, since the whole subject I am dealing with is about people who *don't* arrive but who, nevertheless, write a great deal about the historical space they are creating, I think it's quite important to do that.

DM: It's important to your book that the people who come are people who come with the English language and that they come at the end of the eighteenth century; they come with eighteenth-century notions of what they may find and, in fact, they try to find those things; and they come with the English language which they have to impose somehow on a landscape which has never known it.

PC: To a degree that's true, but I was interested how the linguistic situation in England in the latter half of the eighteenth century wasn't, as some people have assumed, just a language where Johnson's *Dictionary* had just appeared and Botany reigned supreme. There was enormous fluidity in the way language was working at that time: the way that James Cook used names in naming islands and coastlines was quite different from the way Banks understood the use of names. So, I'm a bit reluctant to say that there was, in fact, an imposition on the landscape. I don't really see that the newcomers were better or worse in this respect than anybody else naming the land. The names were provisional, occasional: they were historical events. They defied the attempts of the newcomers to make ready-made places.

The names are extraordinary: Cape Catastrophe, Mount Dromedary, Lake Disappointment. These are names which have to do with *not* finding places; they allude to the inability of English to impose itself easily, and in that sense they are telling us a lot about the history of the people arriving, and about the way they have to renegotiate language itself. I see a much more creative role for the naming process: it's not simply a blank landscape that's written over, it's something that has to be named *in order to be brought into existence*, but its very naming then reflects on the language which is used. Hence 'mountain' refers to a thing which is not there; 'river' refers to something not there.

The names work, but in the course of it they make language very ironic: people go to places which don't exist as a result. So you'll have names like Dry River or Mount Hopeless where what is being said is that, although to all intents and purposes this is a thing we can call a 'river' or a 'mount', in fact it offers us none of the things that word should imply; the landscape is brought into being as a place where language doesn't work.

Obviously this means we can't think about objective eighteenth-century empirical scientists marching methodically across the landscape – what we can see them doing instead is reflecting on the tools and techniques to hand and in fact deviating from the straight and narrow into endless zig-zag routes, both literally and rhetorically, as they try to make sense of what they are finding. All of that precedes what is conventionally called the history of the country.

As soon as you start to talk about the way travelling and writing about travelling *don't* occur in a straightforward linear fashion, as if the country were already there, it also starts to throw light on the whole question of the explorers themselves – what kind of characters they were, what they were doing. If you think of the country as a stage on which certain tragic or comic events were acted out, you are going to place the burden for justifying these mistakes – mistakes commemorated in names like Lake Disappointment or Mount Hopeless – entirely on the shoulders of the explorer: why did the explorer make these mistakes?

It becomes inevitable that you think in terms of his psychology. He was insensitive to local signs, inadequately prepared; he was just another example of the gross European coming to a delicate continent and, once again, showing his inability to adapt. We get that kind of argument coming up time and again and, to offset it, we then have the myth of the hero, somebody who, against overwhelming odds, including his own stupidity, somehow wins through.

DM: He's also a tragic hero in that Renaissance, Aristotelian sense of having some kind of fatal flaw. It's as if we really want all our heroes to be in a way Shakespearean heroes. It's quite interesting that you have two figures in the book that you are obviously quite interested in – Sir Thomas Livingston Mitchell and Matthew Flinders. They're both people who have been written about a great deal biographically in terms of their 'tragedy', as if the mistakes they made derived from character. It's not that you are not interested in character – it seems to me you are – but you are interested in a different notion of character from the Shakespearean one. What's going on in those characters as they explore is for you not a moral drama, but an acting out of the way they interpret the world.

PC: Yes, the conventional way of thinking about a journey is to imagine it already finished: we start from somewhere because we are going to get somewhere else. There's a parallel here with how much biography is written: we start off with the place where the person was born, the environment and hereditary influences; then we move through childhood and adolescence into adulthood. The biography is conceived of as a narrative where the early influences are clearly related to what the person becomes. In other words, it was all foretold and the biographer simply recovers the lost track of time, the track that lies behind the person.

What I wanted to say was that, much by analogy with the kind of history I am writing (which is a history of mapping the world ahead), we should think about the biography of the explorers, not in terms of a set of influences, which are already there, but rather in terms of the explorers' orientation towards the world ahead. How did they see it? Why did they name it in the way they did? Why did they take this route rather than another? Instead of seeing this all as being acted out on a stage and as being subsidiary to some kind of fatal flaw, maybe *this* was their history: this was what they were actually doing. This was why they were explorers.

Instead of going back and taking comfort in something called psychology or environment, we might instead try to understand why they wrote these enormous journals about finding nothing, why they thought it mattered to write what I call a biography of the journey. By looking at how they went about this historical writing, by recognizing it as historical and not as merely of biographical interest, we might cease to feel the need to turn these rather enigmatic figures who make a lot out of nothing into, as you say, heroes or villains.

DM: That's very well brought out in the contrast you make between Cook and Flinders. It is not that you are averse to the idea of character, but you are interested in how it exhibits itself in the working of a mind. You are also interested in the *differences* between characters. There's a splendid contrast between Cook and Flinders:

> Cook, by suspending judgement, had allowed inexplicable novelties, departures from the normal, to appear. Flinders went one step further and *anticipated* them. He adopted an expectant attitude; he looked for signs of change in the belief that the contrast they made with what was already known was itself a source of comparison. It was associative reasoning itself that drew the explorer on. Like a ship at sea, the explorer advanced on the current of his own reasoning. By his mental attitude he attracted the world to him; and, vice versa, he found himself oriented towards the magnetic north of discovery. (*The Road to Botany Bay*, p. 190)

And then another passage where, I think, you want to talk about what is unique to Flinders and to get to the centre of a man in a very moving way – which is not through moral drama:

> as I have already suggested, the significance of these differences [between explorers] is to be sought less in individual psychology than in differing attitudes towards the getting of knowledge.

– and that's the real difference between the way you approach those people and the way other writers do –

> Where such travellers disagreed, it was not so much (or not simply) because of a personality clash, but because they differed over the proper objects of knowledge.
>
> It is at this level, I think, that we need to turn to Flinders's Spencer Gulf place names – not as personal advertisements but as testimonies to a geographical intuition, to a sense that something *objective* linked the traveller to the place he had discovered, and not just the accident of his being first there. When we explore them in this way, something else emerges: we also begin to see how, after all, geographical knowledge was personal knowledge and, in the naming and description of places, it was possible to intimate the very ground of one's own identity. (ibid., p. 181)

It's that perception I want to draw attention to – that the way people orientate themselves geographically, the way they move through a landscape, which you call their geographical intuition, is as unique as any other characteristic, and it may be *that* aspect of exploration that allows us into their characters.

PC: I tried also to say in the book that character (even if it is understood conventionally as a set of virtues and vices, a set of actions which add up to a story) changed. It wasn't simply that there was a contrast between Cook and Flinders in temperament: it was also that, between the time in which Cook was living and working and writing (in the 1770s) and the time that Flinders was writing (in the early 1800s), there were certain subtle changes in the notion of what it was to have an identity.

Whereas for the earlier generation there was a sense in which identity was a more straightforward question – the idea of how you understood the world was a simpler one: you understood it through experience – for Flinders, who was well read in the new psychology and cites poets like Coleridge who promoted it, you didn't simply see the world: you understood it *associatively*.

The question is, what did that mean? Did it simply mean, as some historians have said, that the Europeans came to Australia and changed everything simply because, by the act of association, they reduced everything here to a more or less faithful imitation of what was there? I think not; I think that the new psychology had the effect of placing the observer himself in a quite new position. With Flinders, for instance, the whole question of *where* he was in relation to the object of knowledge was as essential as locating the object of knowledge itself. He had to create a place from which to write quite as much as a place about which to write.

This was quite different from Cook – and that's why we can talk about Flinders biographically, because he in fact understood that his great *Voyage to Terra Australis* was a biography. That book, composed in Mauritius during the seven years the French detained him there on his way back to England, was the writing – the mapping even – of a life; it translated a fairly modest addition to geographical knowledge into a place which embodies his fate.

DM: And it is essentially, to use a word you're quite keen on, 'reflective'. That's the other thing: it goes back over the material in a reflective way.

PC: Yes, and that's why he is pivotal to the book. I try to place him in a position where we see that the question of the language you use and the space it conjures up are interrelated. It's not that one describes another; they constantly reflect on each other. The fact that Flinders effectively created a new genre – the journal as a biography of the journey, with its extraordinary detail and its unashamed addition of a whole volume of personal anecdote to do with his imprisonment in Mauritius – this is a turning-point, not only in my book, but in the development of the literature of exploration. It's here in the book that we start to realize that the way in which you write is instrumental in creating the country you want to inhabit.

DM: Flinders is a character in your writing you obviously feel some affection for and some affinity with?

PC: Certainly, some reviewers have assumed the strength of the chapter derives from a vicarious identification with the biographical subject. I have to say that I don't quite see it like that. I have, actually, visited Flinders's birthplace in Lincolnshire, and spent quite a time wandering around the area in an attempt to try to see whether I could sense any spirit of place in his writing.

DM: Yes, I don't mean that, I mean an affinity of mental outlook. His shifting and provisional way of looking at things seems to be very much your way of wanting to come to grips with things.

PC: Yes, I'm very much drawn to that aspect of his writing. One criticism of the book, which I am sure will go on, is that it seems to make a great deal of what is in fact almost invisible, very hard to see, in conventional historical terms.

DM: That sounds just like Flinders.

PC: Exactly. That's the point. Just because these things cannot be easily translated into conventional biography or conventional stage history, it doesn't mean to say they are not there. It simply means that we have to rethink what we mean by character and destiny.

DM: I must say I was very taken with that Flinders character, as outlined in the passage I read – because that notion of dealing with space as a way of talking about identity is something that is not limited simply to an explorer but is something that people often have to deal with in their daily lives. Whether they could spell it out in quite those terms is another matter.

PC: Well, in your book *12 Edmonston Street*, there's clearly a very interesting sense in which the *place* constructs the *person*, but the place is not there before the writing of it. In other words, if I'm interpreting it properly, the process of recollecting what is there occurs precisely through the writing of a place. Only when one has that *writing place* has one got the autobiographical experience. The autobiographical experience isn't conjured up by going back, in a tourist way, to look at the verandah, the underpinnings of the house: it emerges in the writing of those places, their transformation into, literally, memory places.

DM: Do you think Australians, because of the provisional nature of the continent – the sense in which we feel we don't know it and are always walking a little bit into something unknown – do you think Australians have a particular sensitivity to the notion of mapping spaces? It does seem to me to turn up in a great deal of Australian writing.

PC: Perhaps before answering that, there's something else we should touch on.
There's a very strong presence throughout *The Road to Botany Bay* which comes from the way in which the Aborigines have been left out of that mapping experience. Or, rather, how much of the mapping has been supposed to take place over empty ground or blank space. Aboriginal names, if they were ever sought, have become impossible to render, their routes have become impossible to recover. As a result, we've taken upon ourselves the burden of mapping the country. I think one of the reasons,

as I say in the book, why the identification with the country seems to be so fragile is not just that very often there are not names for the country, but there is a sense in which the country is not felt to be there already, as something which has been intentionally willed, something which a previous generation made sense of. Rather, there's a sense that this writing might have occurred in another way: we might have gone by another route. (In reality, of course, it seems that the historical space we have written for ourselves was a translation, it wasn't an original text.)

So, I would agree with you that some of our poets and novelists are very preoccupied with the question of place and, I guess, my reservation would be that I wonder whether they have misconstrued the nature of those places and have overlooked the fact that they already existed, not just through the naming acts of earlier explorers, but because they themselves (the explorers) were writing over, translating, appropriating earlier histories.

DM: That brings up the question of communication, doesn't it? If the Aborigines had attempted to produce a map that would have been useful to the settlers, they would have produced something that we wouldn't recognize as mapping at all. They might have been 'singing up' the country. It would not have been a map that we could have recognized. And, essential to that lack of recognition would have been language. Like us, they map in language. But in some way what you are saying is that these two languages face each other, and there is no translation between them.

PC: In a sense that's right. But there were translations of course. I think you run a danger in writing a book like this, which deals so much with language as the intermediary between self and world. It's very easy to say that this overlooks the fact that, after all, Aborigines and whites fought each other. It's easy to say: wouldn't it be useful to get back to that empirical space in which spears and bullets were exchanged? Because, unless we do that, we're never going to come to terms with that beginning and that past.

What I would say is that when you do look at those early events, there was a provisional early period of exchange. You can see it in the moment when the Van Diemen's Land settlers came, say, to Port Phillip: according to George Augustus Robinson, the Aboriginal Protector, more than 50 per cent of those early squatters with their sheep were shown the way into the Western District by 'Aboriginal guides'. As I suggest, whether those 'guides' saw themselves in that light is a different matter, but there was a brief historical moment when an Aboriginal landscape was being read by the guide in a way which was quite explicable to those who followed, even though there was very little language communication.

DM: Quite explicable? You often say that what the Aborigines were doing was leading people along a boundary between tribes, a safe place, and that becomes a track for the whites. You also say that the whites were less interested in the track, and where it led, than in the country on either side. You yourself point out that the two peoples were looking at very different things – and in different ways.

PC: Yes, explicable to themselves, not that they understood what was intended by the other. As you say, the question of language was central to the routes one took.

DM: One is struck by how often the Aboriginal word which we all use as a name in fact means in one dialect or another 'I don't know' or 'What a silly question!'

PC: There's an even subtler point here. We think we know that ironic fact because a collector of languages has come along, say forty years after the explorer first got the name, and asked the surviving members of the tribe what the word really means. And they have replied: 'I don't know.' But *what* is it that they don't know? We can't tell simply by looking at the texts.

But the other point is that the very desire to ask that question is what creates the problem. Again, I talk about this quite a lot. In the interview situation the missionary would ask a question and, of course, would receive, instead of answers, incomprehension.

DM: But also the question may be absurd because there is no answer to that.

PC: Yes, it's also a historical question to do with the authorization of certain historical documents – we need that name to be fixed because it's going to last hereafter in the surveys.

DM: But also because we name in different ways.

PC: Absolutely. And, as I discuss in the book, it's very interesting to see how early white ethnographers went about dealing with Aboriginal languages. I suggest that their tendency to dismiss those languages, to say they lacked grammar and syntax and even that they lacked the power to name meant that, in a certain sense, those people did not possess the country. And, for that reason, you did not dispossess them. What happened was that you gave the country names which it had always longed for.

The fact that this was totally inaccurate doesn't affect the interesting point that the Europeans thought language was the essential medium of occupation. Force was used but to make it legitimate, it had to be justified in terms of language.

DM: You also make the point that the frontier is really a place where communication takes place, that a frontier is a place where dialogue occurs – that's quite different from the notions of frontier we are used to.

PC: Yes and I analyse a number of settlers' accounts where you can see that. A woman, say, in Gippsland, describing in her memoirs the act of settlement, does so in terms of the creation of small but eloquent boundaries, symbolic places where speech can congregate and memories. She progressively covers a chair, puts a curtain across a window, gets the fence up at the bottom of the paddock. These events, recorded in her diary, actually evoke her history directly in terms of spatial enclosures – and their transgression. For those boundaries don't exist to shut out the bush; the bush becomes an attractive ferny dell at the very moment it is on the other side of the boundary. Definably different from the stump of the mountain ash symbolically preserved inside the garden and domesticated with geraniums, the wilderness beyond now becomes an object which can be described and loved.

DM: You say it becomes a cultural object because it's now on the other side of the fence and can be seen.

PC: Yes, it can be photographed, you can go for walks there – walks which are no longer exploratory, but are now acts of exploratory reminiscence.

DM: So that boundary becomes, not only a way of defining the enclosed from the unenclosed, or the known from the unknown, but a point at which those two things can meet one another and some kind of interaction take place – and that's the sense in which you mean 'communication'.

PC: And apart from this theoretical point about boundaries, their redefinition as points of communication helps to explain a whole set of early observations to do with Aboriginal movements in the early period. It throws light on why, for instance, some of the mission stations were quite consciously set up at boundary points. Those boundary points weren't frontiers but meeting grounds, neutral places where exchanges could occur.

This conception of the boundary is quite different from the idea of the frontier, which must be pushed on mercilessly until all that is outside is obliterated and rendered 'white' – in many senses.

DM: I was just going to ask you one other thing. Clearly, you would never have written this book if you had not come to Australia. Would you have written a book dealing with something like the same subject but in a different context?

PC: Well, when I first came to Australia I was, in fact, finishing off a draft of a book about Venice. That book is specifically looking at what is left out of accounts of Venetian life and art; and what is left out, it seemed to me, was something called historical space – the space of movement and historical action. So there's obviously a genealogy for this book, and it goes back, more broadly, to a sense I have long had that much contemporary writing – historical, critical, and poetic – seems to take for granted the *givenness* of what are really cultural constructions – whether they are buildings or historical texts.

But my interest is not so much to delve behind or beneath those appearances, those cultural objects, but simply, as it were, to look at the interrelations, the living space, the spaces between words, the spaces between buildings. *The Road to Botany Bay* is quite local in its content, but its form . . . the spatial experience of coming here, of reflecting on Venice have no doubt played their part.

DM: You come with that capacity for that subject and then the continent is here like a gift to explore.

PC: But it's impertinent to talk about it biographically.

DM: I was thinking of Flinders and the objective nature of his subjectivity.

PC: I see. There is a sense in which this book is about saying my experience of this country is *not* that it is given, nor that it is peripheral, but that it is simply where I am. And, rather than rationalize the experience of coming here by insisting that Australia is a second place, a stand-in for somewhere else, which I don't feel, I accept it's a biographical place for me too.

But can it be that I am the only Englishman who has felt this? Clearly not. Is a sense of language being ill at ease here *and* of a space which remains undeciphered uniquely mine? Clearly not. No, when you start to read the journals of the early travellers, you find a whole host of writers . . .

DM: But there's a wonderful coincidence here, isn't there, between the objective place and your own identity – exactly in the Flinders sense, which makes this a very personal book, as well as a book which is objectively revealing of a place and its life.

PC: I call it an 'essay'; there's meant to be a stylistic and structural component which is my perspective, yes.

NOTES

1 This conversation was commissioned and produced by John Tranter. It was first broadcast in the Australian Broadcasting Corporation programme Radio Helicon on 27 March 1988.

MARY HAMER

Putting Ireland on the map

Maps, no less than any other text, are the agents of change. They create sites for the contestation of meaning. No more than classic realism can a map reproduce the material reality of the terrain that is its subject; it can only represent. And in that act, meaning is constructed and disputed, power relations engaged. Mapping conventions, their signifying practices, though apparently rigorously co-ordinated with material reality, cannot deliver cartographers from their inherent commitment to the creation of a new fiction.

What is more, the very activities of measuring, ordering, regulating, and standardizing, the production of accuracy that is the prerequisite of scale mapping, involve a rigorous shaping of the material world that is at odds with and alien to the forms in which the material world has its prior existence. The features of the map-world can only be recognized by a process of abstraction, the learning of a new language. Map-reading does not draw on bodily experience in a three-dimensional world but on familiarity with representational codes. This might seem too obvious to be worth saying, but it has particular relevance to map-making's political force. An abstracted and standardized representation of terrain challenges direct local experience and removes, as it were, the terrain from the cognitive ownership of those who inhabit it.[1]

This kind of alienation was recognized in a recent paper of Fredric Jameson's: although 'Cognitive mapping' addressed the importance of our ability or rather inability to map or think the late-twentieth-century world (of multinational capitalism) we live in, more than one issue raised in his suggestive argument about space can be explored in terms of the nineteenth-century Ordnance Survey's mapping of Ireland.[2]

The first is the issue of 'cognitive mapping' and alienation, terms and an equation which brings them into relationship drawn from the work of Kevin Lynch in *The Image of the City*.[3] Urban alienation, Lynch claimed, increased in proportion as the built city environment defeated the attempts of inhabitants to form a picture of it in their heads: to map it cognitively. Conversely, the firmly marked central urban monuments of Boston and the inescapable sweep of the Charles river offered sense experience that could be cognitively assimilated to produce a stable inner sense of the city space. The vividness and coherence of the environmental image was singled out as being a crucial condition for the enjoyment and use of the city. Jameson suggests that cognitive mapping might profitably be compared with Althusser's definition of ideology: both offer an imagined relationship to the real relations in which the subject lives. Cognitive mapping is the subject's ideology of space.

In one sense, the famous Ordnance Survey project in Britain could make no intervention in the cognitive mapping processes of the Irish, for the Survey officers were not themselves creating a new environment, only recording a given one. But the very process of their record, as will be seen, involved some modification of that environment: ancient boundaries were not always left undisturbed, place-names were anglicized, either directly or more subtly by the attempt to arrive at spellings that looked acceptable to an English eye. So an official Ireland was produced, an English-speaking one, with its own ideology of Irish space.

The activities of the Ordnance Survey were of course only one example of the development of detailed and comprehensive mapping techniques pioneered by the French in the eighteenth century. These projects, designed for the control of space by bringing it under miniaturizing representation, can be understood as playing a part in the generation of unique forms of space that Jameson attributes, in 'Cognitive mapping' and elsewhere, to capitalism. Jameson cites Foucault's work on prisons as a study of the historical production of space, but makes an important qualification. Where Foucault would relate this production to the articulation of power, Jameson would substitute for 'power' the term 'labour'. It is here that his argument becomes most acutely relevant to the Ordnance Survey map of Ireland, for in the planning of the project, its execution and its final product, the development of specialized and new forms of labour is paramount. The production of a new Ireland is as much a form of capitalism as it is of British imperialism.

We are so used to living in a comprehensively mapped world (and to constructing our own cultural paradigms under the direction of the Michelin Guide) that the political thrust of mapping is more readily apparent in cases from cartographic history.[4] The power of naming, for instance, as a means of taking possession by displacement was clearly understood by John Smith, author of *A Description of New England* (1616). He invited Prince Charles, to whom the work was dedicated, to rename the places on the map which accompanied his text, smoothly identifying the assumption of political control with a missionary and civilizing intention.

> I heare present your highness the description in a map; my humblest is, you would please to change their Barbarous names, for such *English* as posterity may say Prince *Charles*, was their godfather.[5]

Seventeenth-century maps of North America reveal a progressive loss of American Indian names, for which names of English origin are substituted.[6] They offer a record of the colonizing process and of its effects; the relationship between the original culture and the soil is textually unpicked and a new ownership asserted.

Maps, then, may be a means of constituting or of disenfranchising the nation. They bring together language and the soil, the twin elements in which nationalism is rooted according to Fichte. But the representation of national language and national boundaries by mapping is by no means a simple or straightforward undertaking.

Using the native language, for instance, is not necessarily to confirm indigenous time-honoured ownership of the soil. It is power that determines meaning, co-opting fantasies of origin to its own ends. When the Ordnance Survey mapped Ireland, Irish place-names were not displaced but co-opted. They were a major feature of the map but they bore no witness to Irish ownership of the soil. They endorsed, rather, two political facts: the state of Union between Britain and Ireland and the power of the English Protestant landowners, the Ascendancy class, in Ireland. This power, derived from the ownership of land, was both political and economic.

One of the conditions which made this sleight of hand possible was the fact that when the English government authorized the scale mapping of Ireland the language and customs of primitive peoples had become established as an object of study in itself. Until the publication in 1987 of George W. Stocking Jr's *Victorian Anthropology* it had been common to overlook or underestimate the significance of the anthropological studies carried on under the name of 'ethnology' in Britain in the early part of the nineteenth century.[7] Stocking, however, has made it clear that so far from being a period barren of theoretical interest for anthropologists, who had preferred to root their study in the Enlightenment, the ethnographical and ethnological writings of the pre-Darwinian years of the century have by virtue of their human subject matter a great deal in common with the modern discipline of anthropology. Ethnology offered a general scientific framework for the systematic study of the linguistic, physical, and cultural characteristics of dark-skinned, non-European, 'uncivilized' peoples. (The Irish were readily assimilated to this category for since the time of Elizabeth the inhabitants of Ireland had been viewed as hardly less 'savage' than the blacks that English colonists encountered overseas.)[8]

Ethnology, which drew on the evidence of comparative philology and comparative anatomy as well as descriptive accounts of custom, institutions and behaviour, derived its methodology from traditional forms of enquiry like natural history. It was founded on the dichotomy, which now embarrasses many modern anthropologists, between the civilized scholarly observer and the observed, reified, savage other. What is distinct in the work of the earlier period, however, is the commitment, at least the initial commitment, to upholding a particular model of the origins of human society. James Cowles Prichard, known, predictably, as the father of ethnology, was developing the discipline from 1808 till his death in 1848. He made it his life's work to demonstrate that the Bible was right and that human society derived from a single source, i.e. Adam. This meant that the model which Prichard and his associates used to structure their data was a degenerationist one: difference, whether in physical type, religion, political institutions, customs, or language was to be traced, if possible, by reference to a decay from primal unity. It is not difficult to see how a systematized study of the phenomena of Irish life would crystallize around these structures of thought, already settling so usefully into place. In consequence, everything about Irish life that was 'othered' by process of meticulous record was liable to define itself as primitive, if not savage, degenerate: mutely pleading, indeed, for the imperial helping hand of civilized England.

If the assertion of English colonial power was in part achieved through the creation of Ireland as an object of knowledge, the attempt to construct an accurate account of the language and the soil of Ireland is a story of inventive recuperation, of representation endlessly reclaimed for existing power relations. These political effects are, however, the product of the struggle with a material task. My plan is to register the perceived aims of the Ordnance Survey's project as formulated and pursued and the consequences of decisions taken to meet practical problems encountered on the way. This will reveal, among other things, that appeals to efficiency regularly served the interests of existing power relations. Finally I shall consider the look of the finished product and the context of visual representations which helped to determine some of its social meaning.

The mapping of Ireland by the Ordnance Survey authorized in 1824 was a hegemonic enterprise rather than one of crude domination. Although it was conducted by British troops (unarmed − they had to hand in their bayonets before going on survey duty), relied on military discipline for its organization and was funded by the British exchequer, the project worked towards producing a document or text that could represent itself as authentically Irish.[9] Only then could it be seen as the guarantee of the justice and inevitability of the political union between the two countries.

The Act of Union was still a recent fact of political history. Coming into law on 1 January 1801, it had established a legislative union between Ireland and Great Britain. The Irish Parliament having been persuaded with various inducements to vote its own dissolution, one hundred seats in the Commons and twenty-eight seats in the Lords were made available to represent Irish interests at Westminster. This arrangement symbolically, at least, disenfranchised the Catholic population: under the Test Act of 1673 no Roman Catholic could hold public office. In 1829 Catholic Emancipation would be granted, but that was not to relieve the grievance of the Union, on which many of Ireland's ills were blamed. It was only at the election of 1852 that Repeal of the Act of Union was displaced as the major electoral issue in Ireland.

Although the Survey was British-led, Irish opinion and Irish skills were not of course excluded from the work. The Spring Rice committee set up to plan it included many Irish members of Parliament and was headed by one. It formally took the professional advice of Irish surveyors in its deliberations. But the class interests represented were those of the landowners, the most powerful class in a country where political power and wealth derived almost exclusively from land. This meant, in effect, the interests of between 2,000 and 3,000 families of Anglican Protestant persuasion: penal statutes of the 1690s had made it difficult for Catholics to own land and few Protestant dissenters did so on any scale.[10] All the executive power was the landowners'. Wellington, then Master of the Ordnance, was himself born in Ireland into the Protestant Ascendancy and the Lord Lieutenant of Ireland was his elder brother. Thus the interests of the Gaelic-speaking, non-landowning Roman Catholic population were without political representation.

But strategies were developed for their co-option, in order that they should be represented, apparently assenting to the order on which their own dispossession was predicated. Central in this was the inscription of the native past. The Survey was already committed to recording the boundaries of the ancient land divisions, known as townlands, as a prelude to valuation. A special department was set up, employing Irish scholars, to adjudicate between variant spellings and determine the proper form of Irish place names. And field officers were enjoined to collect details of ancient monuments and local legends for the volume of commentary that had conventionally accompanied the graphic text of maps. A new Ireland, and one, as I have suggested, subtly regulated by the discourse of ethnology, was produced. It could not but involve the production of a nation and of a national consciousness.

Official cartography, though never before attempted on such a scale, was not new to Ireland. Even in its early manifestations it was demonstrably an instrument of active appropriation.[11] The first call for systematic mapping arose under Elizabeth. It was associated with the defeat of Gerald Fitzgerald, fifteenth and last Earl of Desmond, who with others in 1579–80 rebelled against Elizabeth and was proclaimed a traitor. After he was caught and killed in 1583 it was decided to confiscate the rebels' lands and to resettle them with loyal colonists brought from the west of England, an enterprise known as the Munster plantation. Even before the lands were divided up it was determined, in line with contemporary developments in the extension of social control, that the transfer should be used to establish a strictly hierarchical social organization, with large estates or 'seignories', each the responsibility of a gentleman 'undertaker' supported by a graded infrastructure of tenant farmers, craftsmen, and labourers.[12] A similar organizational grid was to be applied to the land. Until then measured only by the unstable medieval unit of the ploughland, Irish soil was to submit to standardization in acres, the modern unit that English surveying had adopted. The terrain was also to be analysed, to distinguish different qualities and uses of land and the boundaries between forfeited and unforfeited estates established. An account in graphic form as well as in words was to be made of the confiscated estates. The power of the conqueror was asserted not merely in confiscation and resettlement but in the insistent reduction of the territories to knowableness and fixity.

This was pursued with an arithmetical exactness. It was decided that the unit for measuring the new colony should be the English perch of 16½ feet. The sizes of seignories were fixed at either 4,000, 6,000, 8,000 or 12,000 acres; the number of seignories to be got out of each county was calculated and how many tenant farmers each undertaker should be expected to accommodate. There was even a model drawn up of a possible disposition of demesne, tenant farms and manorial villages on the ideal Munster estate. This does represent the most extreme form of ideological redescription, for its ingenious tessellating of farms in rectangles and triangles was secured at the cost of ignoring all physical variation on the ground. The plan did not get enforced as policy, however, and the articles agreed between government and undertakers in June 1586 were confined to specifications of size; a landlord's tenants should include six farmers with 400 acres each, six freeholders with 300 acres each, and forty-two copyholders with 100 acres each. There were to be at least thirty-six of the smallest farms at 50, 25, or 10 acres.

These new units were to be superimposed on and somehow reconciled with what John Andrews identifies as 'a network of ancient land divisions which were considerably smaller than the new seignories and too firmly grounded in the popular consciousness to be ignored'.[13] Mapping, he suggests, was the gesture of appropriation which would permit the new landlords to take a formal possession of their territories and free them henceforward to accept the native territorial structure. If he is right, this would have secured the double benefit of co-opting the native past and diminishing the likelihood of resistance to the new order. This was to be the strategy of the nineteenth century too.

There had been general agreement for some years that a centralized survey of the whole of Ireland was needed for administrative purposes, when in February 1824 Wellington, Master-General of the Ordnance, agreed that his survey department would be prepared to do the work. This did not in itself constitute the promise of direct action: prompted by an anxiety to ensure that the enterprise was aimed towards what they saw as the significant tasks to be achieved, Thomas Spring Rice and a number of other Irish Members of Parliament collaborated to set up a select committee, which took its first evidence on 22 March 1824. They were above all concerned that the survey should provide for a revaluation of the soil of Ireland with the purpose of putting internal taxation, long a source of grievance and unrest, on a more demonstrably equitable footing.[14] An official delimitation of every townland – ancient territorial divisions, smaller than an English parish – was called for. This was to be followed by an official valuation of the land and buildings within each of these, to be used as the basis for revising the tax known as the county cess. (It was this tax that paid for gaols, court-houses and the salaries of various local officials and for the building and repair of roads and bridges.) On 21 June they made their report and the following day Colonel Thomas Colby, Director of the Ordnance Survey in Britain, was instructed to proceed.

In many ways he had been given an extremely free hand, once the committee had decided that the military were indeed to be entrusted with the job, for its members were not themselves professional cartographers, but landowners in the main. The ambiguity of his task was reflected, however, in the chain of command. Colby was obliged to take his orders from the Master-General and the Board of Ordnance in Pall Mall, yet required to take account of the views of the Irish government on matters affecting domestic policy. He could choose his own subordinates and pretty well order the management of the Survey as he saw fit. The Survey headquarters were set up in Phoenix Park, where he put in Major William Reid as his resident deputy. Staffing was already in hand: Wellington had put twenty cadets into training for the work early in 1824 and by Christmas 1825 there were thirty-five officers. The field work, Reid persuaded Colby, should be done by sappers, although in England civilians were used. This anxiety over Irish competence had to be set aside when insufficient numbers of English could be found to train: at the beginning of 1826, eighty-seven English sappers and fifty-three 'country labourers' were employed. Triangulation had begun in mid-July 1825. In 1828 Lieutenant Thomas Aiskew Larcom was put in charge of a department to engrave and publish the maps at Phoenix Park and by 1846 the last map had been published.[15]

Masquerading as a process of systematic record, the mapping of Ireland was a prolonged act of cultural displacement and textual processing, in the course of which ancient place-names and boundaries were incorporated and reinscribed. The Irish themselves were largely excluded from executive participation in this project, except, significantly, in matters of philological and antiquarian importance. This allowed British control of the process to remain unchallenged, while visibly incorporating specifically Irish knowledge about Ireland. This knowledge, however, of the Irish language and its roots and about the Irish past, took its form from the current discourse of ethnology, and was in its turn a means of placing Ireland (low) on the developmental scale in relation to England. The work of the Survey confirmed the appropriateness of Ireland's subjected status, represented as Union with Great Britain. In this marriage, Ireland was clearly the wife.

The decision to survey Ireland implied a more wholesale investigation and inscription of the country than a modern reader might expect, for by tradition maps were customarily supplemented by written commentaries.[16] Survey officers were instructed to collect information considerably in excess of what was necessary for or could be shown on a map. Apart from the obvious colonialist implications of this subjection to record, the data collected could be used quite specifically, within the discourse of ethnology, as a means of classifying the inhabitants. Thus Larcom instructed field officers to take note of the following features of Irish life:

> Habits of the people. Note the general style of the cottages, as stone, mud, slated, glass windows, one story or two, number of rooms, comfort and cleanliness. Food; fuel; dress; longevity; usual number in a

family; early marriages; any remarkable instances on either of those heads? What are their amusements and recreations? patrons and patrons' days; and traditions respecting them? What local customs prevail, as Beal tinne, or fire on St John's Eve? Driving the cattle through fire, and through water? Peculiar games? Any legendary tales or poems recited around the fireside? Any ancient music, as clan marches or funeral cries? They differ in different districts, collect them if you can. Any peculiarity of costume? *Nothing more indicates the state of civilisation and intercourse.* (my emphasis)[17]

The tenor of these inquiries is not neutral: evidence of squalor, improvidence (the Irish were notorious for their early marriage), aberration and superstition are specifically invited. The ambiguous power of the inscriber is sharply demonstrated in the reference to the Irish past. Writing up ancient customs could represent itself as antiquarian and disinterested but it could with at least equal justice be seen as a means of appropriating that past in order to legitimize the colonized present. Battle for ownership of the Irish past was to be a recurrent feature of attempts to create a national consciousness. It was in fact in 1831, the year after Larcom issued these instructions, that the nationalist politics of James Hardiman's *Irish Minstrelsy; or Bardic Remains of Ireland* provoked a series of hostile review articles in the *Dublin University Magazine*.[18]

'Work', as I have indicated, is a key term in understanding the implications of the Survey. The exclusion of the Irish from the work was in itself a statement of their underdevelopment and the systematized labour which went into the enterprise was represented as a mark of English superiority. During the first half of the nineteenth century, a quite specific notion of work, highly organized on the factory model, was coming to be understood as a mark of civilized life.[19] This was beyond the native Irish, as the words of Richard Colley Wellesley, Lord Lieutenant of Ireland, make plain: 'Neither science, nor skill, nor diligence nor discipline nor integrity sufficient for such a work [as the Survey] can be found in Ireland.'[20] What is absent are the marks of civilized human development (which is equated with the ability to submit to highly organized forms of collaborative labour): this authorizes the intervention of the colonial power. So although Irish witnesses to the committee had advocated a division of labour between soldiers and civilians, the valuation exercise became militarized and the scope for Irish involvement curtailed.

An immediate effect of defining the Irish as incompetent was to depress national achievement. The Spring Rice committee did hint that some local men might be employed but its most powerful recommendation was that all major cartographic projects on small scales should forthwith be abandoned as obsolete. In consequence, the projects of a number of distinguished Irish surveyors were aborted:

Nimmo stopped work on his charts and Griffith on his trigonometrical survey of Munster, while several promising county surveys – Bald's

Clare, Aher's Kilkenny, MacNeill's Louth, Armstrong's Armagh – were never heard of again.[21]

Eschewing and replacing unsystematized private endeavour, the new 6–inch map was to bring the whole colonized space within a single system of representation devised by officers from the English Ordnance Survey.

The discourse of production masked the political force of this decision. It was anticipated that Ordnance officers would be more accurate in their measurements than civilians and because they were trained to work as a unit the committee could leave questions of planning and internal consultation to them; they could also supply cheap skilled labour, for they planned to train surveyors specially for the task and to employ them at a relatively low rate of pay. They had a superior theodolite. Although there had been some hesitation at first, in committing the officers of the Ordnance Survey to mapping Ireland for valuation purposes, a task which had little in common with their regular work of surveying terrain for military reasons, the Spring Rice committee came to argue that considerations of efficiency and economy would best be served that way.

In fact, the attempt to secure efficiency was inevitably in conflict with the stated intention of achieving an accurate material record, as the work of the boundary department testified. It was Richard Griffith, the only Irish engineer to find a place within the new organization of labour, who was appointed to take charge of the new department, charged to mark the boundaries of townlands.[22] The department was empowered to enter private property, but required only to mark boundaries and not to measure them. In theory its work was wholly uncontentious, for the names and outlines of these divisions were assumed to be locally well enough known. It was necessary that they should be publicly marked so that the acreages and relative values could be calculated. In fact, the prospect of the calculations to be performed exercised what many felt was an undue influence on Griffith's practice: not content with recording boundaries, he changed them. He made a policy, on occasion, of amalgamating neighbouring townlands, and he was prepared to join together a group of disparate small areas, traditionally separate, under a single name for convenience. The same principle led him to break up divisions that were too large to be easily valued. Land divisions of long standing and current local practice were not reliably represented even at this preliminary stage.

Applied to language, the effect of the rationalizing administrative principle was plural and unpredictable. Even the use of the designation 'townland' involved imposing a new uniformity, for some parts of Ireland had called these territorial divisions 'ploughland', 'tate' or 'ballibo'. On the whole, however, the boundary department's commitment to reason and efficiency led to the retaining of original place-names, since this would facilitate the continued use of old documents in modern legal proceedings. It also resulted in the Irish form usually being preferred to a modern English version. But because altering some boundaries had created new townlands, some new names had to be created: this was done often by adding 'east', 'west', 'upper', 'lower', etc. to the original. This meant the old documents could still be used and apparent continuity with the past maintained, but it also involved a mechanical anglicization. In so far as Griffith allowed taste rather than reason to guide him, he advised against the adoption of a name like 'Oatencake' in county Cork: there is some trace of an aesthetic or elitist censor at work. What was in theory a transcription was compromised by censorship and redefinition. When it came to deciding on a spelling, however, Griffith did instruct his men to compare the standard sources, the barony constable's list, or landowners' estate maps with the local pronunciation.

The tension between the written and the spoken forms of language focused a problem of evaluation that military surveyors were not equipped to deal with. The slipperiness of language resisted their schemes for arriving at the right or the best answer in a way that the soil did not. The boundary department's version of local names was not final. It was only one of the authorities that district engineer officers were enjoined to collect in their local 'namebooks' for central scrutiny: these might include local landowners, agents, clergy and schoolmasters, county records and existing maps. (It is important not to overlook the exclusionary nature of this list. The power of naming is restricted, by implication, to those with authority over the land or to those with a special responsibility for transmitting values enshrined in written language. Printed sources are preferred over manuscript ones. Andrews particularly notes the absence of reference to modern widely circulated materials such as advertisements, newspapers, and directories.) The early policy of adopting whichever version was recommended by the majority of sources seemed to be based on the hope of defining some quantitative measure of orthographical 'correctness'. Yet even this principle could not be applied without contradiction because for generations Irish place-names had already been variously distorted through the pronunciation of English-speaking settlers. This meant that the majority principle produced different spellings of what even a non-specialist could tell were actually the same place-name elements – such as Drum, Drim or Drom, a ridge. In 1829 a field officer of 'C' district identified the problem, admitting that there was no one right name but a contest between tongues. He asked whether it should be the 'original and descriptive Irish name' or 'the one generally received and spelt'. The question at once defines the ancient language as the site of meaning and distinguishes it from the modern written form of everyday usage. The effect is both to privilege and to alienate the past.

A special topographical department had been set up to collate the evidence of old records, current Irish speech and contemporary authorities with regard to place-names. By no means indifferent to the claims of etymology, Major Larcom, the director of the Survey, had first tried to learn the Irish language himself before taking the decision in 1830 to appoint an Irish scholar and a special department of topography briefed to research the original Irish form of names. After all the work of comparison and research to arrive at a form for which purity, accuracy, or authenticity could be claimed, the spelling recommended by the topographical department might be found to differ from every other known form of the name. Attempts, rational in themselves, to regularize spelling and relate it to pronunciation and meaning, often succeeded only in intervention. Forty-six in a random sample of one hundred townland names of Irish derivation were found to differ from all recorded authorities. And because the overwhelming majority of those who would be using the maps were English-speaking, the Survey tolerated inexact renderings of Irish pronunciation in order to achieve a written form that would not look too outlandish to English readers.[23]

This conflict between apparent respect for the Irish language and a readiness to remodel it to suit the convenience of those who did not speak it reflected a tension that was reiterated throughout the work of the Survey. But there was a sense in which investigating the Irish language was a special case: an organized discipline devoted to the study of language through comparative linguistics was already in place and the terms of that wider discourse would inevitably prevail. Philology, however, was a highly politicized field, using hierarchy as a means of organizing difference as Edward Said and others have demonstrated.[24] It was used not just as a means of comparing languages. Language became a test of race and a means of evaluating cultures.

The original hypothesis that the Sanskrit, Latin, Greek, Persian, German and Celtic languages derived from a common ancestor, made by Sir William Jones in 1786, had been subsequently developed, largely by German scholars, to produce a hierarchy of languages with the Germanic languages at its head. The superiority of the Germanic peoples and ways of life was thereby implied. The Celtic were produced as subsidiary. This is reflected in the title of Franz Bopp's 1816 study *On The Conjugational System of the Sanskrit Language in Comparison with that of the Greek, Latin, Persian, and Germanic Languages*, from which the Celtic is omitted. It is true that J. C. Prichard reinstates it, in his 1831 work *The Eastern Origins of the Celtic Nations Proved by a Comparison of their Dialects with the Sanskrit Greek, Latin and Teutonic Languages* but Prichard also had an axe to grind. His own name suggests a Welsh and therefore Celtic origin. Furthermore, it was his aim to make use of philology to support the monogenist account of Creation offered by Genesis. The model he and other biblical anthropologists were using was degenerationist, as indicated above: the human race and human language had been first established in a unitary form from which present difference was derived.[25] Connecting the Celts through language with a primary human origin did not necessarily work to their advantage. The contemporary decay of their country, noted with such distress by English travellers, showed how far the Celtic race had declined from their original parity with other nations.

For the English, time-honoured deprecation of the Celt could now be put on a scientific basis. It is clear that any philological study incorporated in the work of the Survey could only by implication confirm the inferior status of Ireland's Celtic-speaking inhabitants. In fact, *The Townland Index*, published in 1862 as a guide to place-names, does contain in its Preface a considerable body of philological material, very similar in its methodology to Prichard's and clearly offered as a guarantee of the soundness of the work done and its commitment to the Irish past.

The knowledge of Ireland collected by the officers of the Survey had extended enormously beyond the work of measurement and naming involved in the original brief. It became a work of ethnography on the grand scale. Even though all the material collected in that vast project could not be published – there was to be no *Description of Ireland* to rival the French *Description de l'Egypte* (1809–28) – that was not the point: the lives of the Irish people had been opened out to view, had been inspected, enumerated, inscribed, and assessed. *The Townland Index* demonstrated what a wholesale process of standardization that had been. The body of the *Index* consisted of a tabulated inventory of the whole country and a guide to its administrative divisions, setting out in alphabetical order,

> the name of every Townland, TOWN and *Island* mentioned in the census publications, and the number of the Sheet of the Maps of the Ordnance Survey in which the several denominations are to be found; also the area of each Townland, and the County, Barony, Parish, and Poor Law Union in which it is situated. The volume and page of the Townland Census, from which information may be procured as to the Population, and Houses, in 1841 and 1851, and the Poor Law Valuation, in 1851, are also given.
> The Townland names are printed in Roman characters, the TOWNS in small CAPITALS, and *Islands*, which are *not* Townlands in *Italics*.[26]

Such a transformation of the colonized into discourse has implications beyond the instrumental, as Edward Said has demonstrated. In such a process the colonized is typically passive and spoken for, does not control its own representation but is represented in accordance with a hegemonic impulse by which it is constructed as a stable and unitary entity. This is not all: bringing it within the confines of knowledge, making it knowable, robs the colonized, as Said claims, of contradiction and depth, to be left drained and empty under the gaze of the conqueror.[27] This emptiness may be reflected in the very look of the finished large-scale map with its fine lines tracing an open white space.

It is the look of the map in general that I want to consider now. Its most striking characteristic is its emptiness. If Andrews writes appreciatively in *Irish Maps* of its austere beauty, in *A Paper Landscape* he admits to its frequent 'disagreeably naked and anonymous [effect], like an outline engraver's exercise, in extreme cases, rather than a piece of real countryside'.[28] The truth was that though enormous care was expended on setting up a mechanism to divide the tasks of the Survey and to provide for the work of each department to be cross-checked by another,

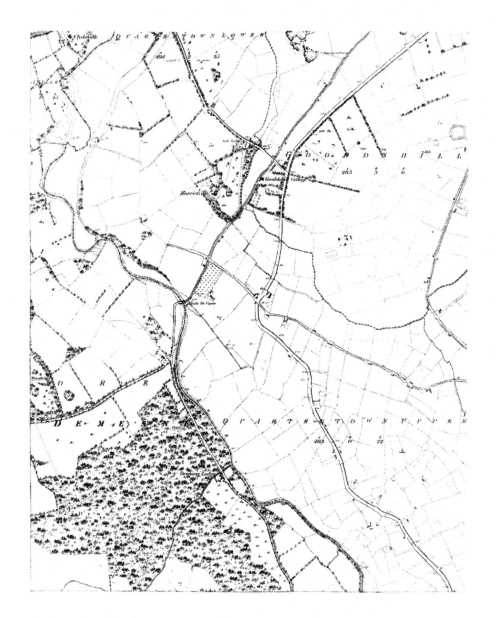

Syndics of Cambridge University Library.

an elaborately systematized division of labour on the industrial model, instructions about what the finished map should actually look like had from the first been few. The chief purpose of the enterprise was a survey and valuation of land rather than the production of a map and so the linear representation might with justice be described as its unconscious product.

One reason why the map looked so empty was the scale on which it was drawn. Andrews, uncharacteristically, attaches considerable symbolic significance to the adoption of the 6-inch scale. To him it is clear that it was its familiarity to the Survey officers rather than its appropriateness to the Irish map that secured its use:

> Whatever its origins, by 1824 the 6-inch scale had established a place for itself in Ordnance Survey thinking, and there is nothing in Colby's evidence to the Spring Rice committee to suggest that his decision was dictated by any close knowledge of peculiarly Irish circumstances. *It should rather be regarded as a cartographic expression of the union of the two kingdoms, comparable with the act (passed while the committee was at work) for extending statute measure to Ireland.* (my emphasis)[29]

The 6-inch scale in itself confirmed the Union. In practical terms it was a choice that gave scope for considerable detail, but the Spring Rice committee, having agreed to it, made no proposals about format and restricted themselves to two recommendations about subject matter – the heights of the principal mountains and the boundary of unenclosed lands.[30] They unequivocally rejected field boundaries, the sort of cartographic detail appropriate to the scale (and shown on the Ordnance Survey's own maps of southern England); Andrews concludes that it was Spring Rice's own fear that a map of existing fences would do harm by publicizing the low state of Irish agriculture that determined their exclusion.[31] Recognizing the incompleteness of his brief, and that he risked having a large-scale map with few details, Colby asked Wellington's opinion, to be advised that 'the map must be drawn and filled up on the scale of six inches to a mile'. It fell to Colby to interpret this and to modify the Survey's practice as occasion required.[32]

If there was uncertainty about what material features to include, the map did succeed in representing social relations within the nation. Some unreflecting practices adopted by the Survey reinforced class structures and signalled class rather than national ownership of the land. Something that appropriated significance for itself in the maps was the demesnes of the gentry, the land around the big houses. Landowners were allowed to be the sole source of authority for the name of their demesnes and were allowed to define their own demesne boundaries: the effect of this was to change the function of the survey in such cases, from marking the land to bearing witness to its ownership.

One of the features of the map is its uncompromising lack of colour. The discipline of the Ordnance Survey's practice is reflected in the plainness of the black and white map, more like a page of print than a picture. In the process of drawing up the map there was some thought of colour. Colby did create a colour code to be used on the ground in the manuscript stage: carmine for brick and stone houses, black for cabins, water in blue, bleach-greens in green, altitude figures in red, and demesnes in various shades. A plan to print contours in blue or brown came to nothing, however, and a simple line of fine dots was adopted. It may in the end have been Colby's own distaste for colour that determined the bleaching of the final engraved form.

Not only colourless, the maps because of their scale have a curiously spaced-out quality, like an expanded close-up, which makes it hard for the perception to grasp them, in Andrews's words, as a piece of real countryside. They have the look, rather, of cells under a microscope: lines traced about largely empty spaces. This resemblance is not anachronistic, for it was in the 1820s that the cell became clearly visible, thanks to the introduction of improved microscopes, and in the second quarter of the century that cell theory was developed. Nor is it one to pass over, for it directs us towards Foucault's analysis, in *The Order of Things*, of the effects of focusing concentrated observation, including the use of microscopes, on natural phenomena.[33] What he has to say about the way observation and language were brought together in the natural history of the seventeenth-century taxonomists and the effective constitution of new knowledge has a bearing for our understanding of the 6-inch map of Ireland. As Foucault describes it, this discourse in which the visible is newly constituted through language has close affinities with the activity of mapping on a large scale: 'The area [of visibility] defines natural history's condition of possibility, and the appearance of its screened objects: lines, surfaces, forms, reliefs.' The screened objects on the slide are the topography of a restricted world. (In this world, too, dictating a change of scale is important in securing discursive authority.) Not all that is visible, however, as he is quick to point out, is capable of being utilized. The essence of the discipline is observation, the attempt to see systematically. Colour, especially, can scarcely serve as a basis for useful comparison. The area of visibility is thus restricted to black and white.

In the discourse of natural history, termed by Foucault 'the nomination of the visible', he asserts that language was brought as close as possible to the observing gaze, with two effects: it was thus possible to exclude uncertainty and to arrive at 'a description acceptable to everyone'.[34] The latter assertion concerning the power of systematized vision is of obvious relevance to the political force of the new map. If natural history produces a vision which 'can be analysed, recognised by all and thus given a name that every one will be able to understand', so does the black and white scale map with its painstaking elaborations of exactitude produce an Ireland that can be universally acceptable and recognized by all: the very definition of a hegemonic text.

In addition, the association with microscope-viewing had particular implications for the nineteenth-century gazing public. Lister's development of the achromatic objective transformed the social meanings attached to the instrument and the world it revealed. The microscope had previously been a source, indeed, a focus of anxiety, because it was difficult to use – distortion of shape and colour could not be avoided and it was hard to adjust – while the suspicion lingered that the lens created the organisms it revealed. G. H. Lewes took this fear seriously enough to claim it was the reason some nineteenth-century physiologists 'still scorned the use of the microscope'.[35] After the 1830s, however, the new microscopes became enormously popular: microscopical societies were formed (the London one in 1840), specialist publications issued, soirées and conversaziones devoted to looking down them. More surprisingly, their enhanced accuracy was to some extent taken as the guarantee of a stability their use could impart to the social formation. This derived from the wholesomeness of the visions (texts?) they offered, and the evidence of divine order they disclosed. Looking down a microscope let you see things more as God did: 'And what can be a more worthy occupation, than the attempt to gain an insight, however limited, into the operations of Creative Wisdom?'[36] Looking down a microscope might help you to fulfil your marriage vows:

> The microscope made or revealed all nature as vocal with praise to its Divine Artificer. What more appropriately could be brought into the family circle. Amidst the drifting storms of winter and the burning heats of summer, in sickness and in health, in riches and in poverty the microscope was the endless medium of amusement and instruction.[37]

It was even hoped that the microscope might serve as a means of social control: getting the poor to look down them might help to avert the threat posed by their vitality, seen as prompt to slide into 'grovelling sensuality'.[38] Slides, by imaging God's organization, promoted social cohesion: a map that looked like a slide might claim some part in representing divine order and promoting peace on earth by keeping people quiet.

But it is not just the diagrammatic qualities of these maps that determine their power. Naming and measuring endorse what is graphically represented. Twice, on each side of the foot of each large sheet, the scale, showing the relation of chains and perches to the mile, is set out. In the right-hand corner the date (14 October 1844) that the map was received from the engraver is noted. The Survey did not just engrave the names by which it was electing to recommend that places should be known, but the names of the men to be credited with producing the finished map. Thus, centred at the foot of the sheet in miniscule copperplate, Sheet 34, county Cork, bears the legend:

> Surveyed 1841–42 by Major Waters & Captains Tucker & Rimington & Lieuts James & Stace R.E. & Engraved in 1844 under the direction of Captain Larcom R.E. AT THE ORDNANCE SURVEY OFFICE PHOENIX PARK by Willm. Walker & Jas. Menzies, the Ornament by

Wm Archibald, the Writing by P. Frazer; Colonel Colby F.R.S.L. & E.M.R.I.A. & Superintendent.

By its precision of dating, its hierarchy and its reinforcement of civilian subordination to military authority, the notice guarantees the integrity of the representation. It also confirms a subjected status. What is recorded is the work of the colonist. And difference, whether issuing in variation in place-names, in the clash of Irish and English surnames, or in the variety of colour, has been cancelled. Ireland has been investigated and reduced to a single universal formula. And that, the left-hand corner declares, is 'Published and sold on behalf of Her Majesty's Government'.

Homerton College, Cambridge

NOTES

I should like to thank the staff of Cambridge University Library's Map Room, Aaron Klug for encouragement and information at an early stage and Terence Hawkes for sustained editorial advice, including directing me towards the idea of cognitive mapping.

1 An illustration of this: Trollope, when he wrote *Castle Richmond*, his third Irish novel, set it very precisely in the area around Mallow. It was an area in which he had himself lived for some years: the place-names he makes use of are the names of real settlements in that area. But it is not possible to find all of them on the same map. Differences of size mean that some do not register on a scale map that shows the largest. It was necessary to conflate maps of different scales in order to include all the places named in the novel for the forthcoming World's Classics edition, places through which the body moves without impediment.
2 Fredric Jameson, 'Cognitive mapping', in Gary Nelson and Lawrence Grossberg (eds), *Marxism and the Interpretation of Culture* (London: Macmillan, 1988), pp. 347–57.
3 Kevin Lynch, *The Image of the City* (Cambridge, Mass.: MIT Press, 1960).
4 See *Word and Image*, 4, 2 (1988), 'Maps and Mapping', especially G. N. G. Clarke, 'Taking possession: the cartouche as cultural text in eighteenth-century American maps', pp. 455–74; William Boelhower, 'Inventing America: a model of cartographic semiosis', pp. 475–97; Stephen Bann, 'The truth in mapping', pp. 498–509.
5 Quoted Clarke, op. cit., p. 457.
6 Quoted Boelhower, op. cit., p. 494.
7 George W. Stocking, Jr, *Victorian Anthropology* (New York: Free Press, 1987).
8 ibid., p. 234; R. N. Lebow, *White Britain and Black Ireland* (Philadelphia: Institute for the Study of Human Issues, 1976).
9 Brian Friel, John Andrews, and Kevin Barry, '*Translations* and *A Paper Landscape*', *Crane Bag*, 8, 2 (1983), pp. 118–24.
10 David Cairns and Shaun Richards, *Rewriting Ireland* (Manchester: Manchester University Press, 1988), p. 23; I have drawn repeatedly on this work.

11 Here and throughout my argument I draw extensively on the publications of J. H. Andrews: *Ireland in Maps* (Dublin: Dolmen Press, 1961); *A Paper Landscape* (Oxford: Clarendon Press, 1975); *Irish Maps* (Dublin: Eason & Son, 1975); *Plantation Acres* (Belfast: Ulster Historical Foundation, 1985).

12 Andrews, *Plantation Acres*, pp. 28–46.

13 ibid., p. 32.

14 Andrews, *A Paper Landscape.*, p. 21.

15 ibid., pp. 21, 35–9.

16 Andrews, *A Paper Landscape*, pp. 144–5.

17 ibid., p. 148. See also below, note 19.

18 Cairns and Richards, *Rewriting Ireland*, pp. 28–9 and *passim.*

19 See 'The problem of civilisation in England', in *Victorian Anthropology*, pp. 30–6. In the wake of the French Revolution the definition of the political and economic conditions of a fully civilized life became a major aim. Issues of economics, politics, morality, and class converged in this discussion. The result was that after 1830 'civilization' often tended to imply a number of things that were rather specific reflections of recent British experience: Stocking lists 'the factory system and free trade; representative government and liberal political institutions; a middle-class standard of material comfort and the middle-class ethic of self-discipline and sexual restraint; and the Christian religion in its protestant form.'

20 Andrews, *A Paper Landscape.*, p. 21.

21 ibid., pp. 33–4.

22 The boundary department had not been set up as a part of the Ordnance Survey but to be directly responsible to the lord-lieutenant at Dublin Castle. It was thus not under the jurisdiction of the military but was answerable to the local representative of English rule: if not part of the Ordnance, it did derive its authority from England.

23 Andrews, *A Paper Landscape*, p. 125.

24 Cairns and Richards, *Rewriting Ireland*, pp. 44–5; Edward Said, *Orientalism* (London: Routledge & Kegan Paul, 1978), pp. 131, 133.

25 Stocking, *Victorian Anthropology*, p. 49.

26 *The Townland Index* (London: Agricultural and Emigration Statistics Office, 1861), p. 2.

27 Said, *Orientalism*, pp. 83–7, 255–83.

28 Andrews, *A Paper Landscape*, p. 121.

29 ibid., p. 24.

30 ibid., p. 23.

31 ibid., pp. 30–1.

32 ibid., p. 57.

33 L. J. Rather, P. Rather, and J. B. Frerichs, *Johannes Müller and the Nineteenth-Century Origins of Tumour Cell Theory* (Canton, Mo: Science History Publications, 1986), pp. 1–56; Michel Foucault, *The Order of Things* (London: Tavistock Publications, 1970), pp. 132–8.

34 Foucault, op. cit., p. 134.

35 Quoted in Stella Butler, Olivia Brown, and R. H. Nuttall, *The Social History of the Microscope* (Cambridge: Whipple Museum of the History of Science, 1986), p. 2.

36 ibid., p. 5.

37 ibid., p. 7.

38 ibid.

PETER NICHOLLS

Futurism, gender, and theories of postmodernity

Why Futurism? From the perspective of Anglo-American Modernism, the Italian movement has tended to seem transparent in its extremism and, perhaps for that reason, merely an opening phase in a larger sequence of avant-garde initiatives. This pigeon-holing of Futurism is, of course, one consequence of that history of Modernism which the Modernists themselves were so keen to write – we recall Wyndham Lewis's scornful dismissal of Marinetti's 'automobilism' and Ezra Pound's rejection of the new aesthetic as merely 'accelerated impressionism'.[1] Clearly polemical, such comments may now strike us as also being somewhat superficial; certainly, they prevent us from seeing the extent to which Italian Futurism provided a kind of ideological force-field which successive avant-gardes could oppose but not ignore.

I want to argue here that in its celebration of modernity, Futurism proposed a view of capitalism whose extreme implications were to a large extent obscured by the dismissive (and non-political) interpretations of the Anglo-American avant-garde. For modernization, as it was hailed by Marinetti and his colleagues, amounted to more than a series of stunning technological innovations; it entailed the extension of the market, the penetration of capital into spaces hitherto resistant to it. Those spaces might be literal, geographical ones (hence the strong imperialist thrust to Marinetti's propaganda) or they might be psychological and imaginative ones, the province of interiority itself. The commitment to expansionism in early Futurist theory thus had both highly specific political motivations (the desire to throw off the yoke of the Triple Alliance, the need to solve the problem of the *mezzogiorno* through the opening of new labour opportunities abroad), and others which were more general as they were more closely allied with a metaphysics of the modern (the increasing momentum of monopoly capitalism as the sign of a collective, 'cosmic' experience of the new). In that sense, Futurism conceived modernization as a relentless overcoming of resistance, a destruction of those differential and dialectical formations in culture which threatened to impede the homogenizing movements of capital. Questions of gender and subjectivity were insistently problematic here, and the Futurists found ways of resolving them which provided an almost automatic point of reference for other Modernist innovations, and which, so I shall argue, may also supply a kind of subtext to recent theories of postmodernity.[2]

I

The basic elements of Italian Futurism are best known from the first manifesto of 1909. There Marinetti proposed an aesthetic founded on speed, violence, and the machine; in doing so he also expressed the avant-garde stance in what was to be its definitive form: 'No work without an aggressive character can be a masterpiece.'[3] Marinetti's celebration of modernity, a conflation of a dionysian primitivism with the new energies of the technological age, also specifies those institutions which stand in the way of modernization: 'We will destroy the museums, libraries, academies of every kind, will fight moralism, feminism, every opportunistic or utilitarian cowardice.'[4] Why should feminism be included in this list? The most notorious proposal in the manifesto reads: 'We will glorify war – the world's only hygiene – militarism, patriotism, the destructive gestures of freedom-bringers, beautiful ideas worth dying for, and scorn for woman.'[5] This 'scorn for woman' was to permeate the thought of other Modernist avant-gardes, and it clearly amounted to something more than either a class-based misogyny or an attempt to promote a 'manly' sense of pride in Italy's technological and imperialist potential. For a recurrent theme in Modernist polemic – a theme given definitive form in the Futurist manifestos – is that Woman is 'anti-modern', that the feminine denotes a particular psychological formation which is in some way resistant to the new.

On one level, of course, the Futurist contempt for 'feminine' values arose from an attack on the outmoded social structures of Italian society. This explains a set of fundamental contradictions in Marinetti's various pronouncements, for along with the outspoken chauvinism for which he is well-known there developed an equally outspoken propaganda on behalf of feminist concerns. The so-called 'Manifesto of the Futurist Political Party' (1918) numbers among its main proposals the facilitation of divorce, universal suffrage, and the right to equal salaries; elsewhere Marinetti mounted a bitter critique of the family which he saw as little better than 'a legal prostitution powdered over with moralism.'[6]

The Futurist 'scorn for women' was thus rather more complicated than it has often seemed, for it was closely related to the Nietzschean desire for a transcendence of the 'merely' human. From that perspective, Marinetti saw past cultures (and Italian culture in particular) as locked into social and psychological roles which were deeply repressive. He could thus afford to be quite ambivalent about the 'woman question' since the principal Futurist objective was ultimately 'the creation of a non-human type.'[7] Although Marinetti's fantasy of a new heroic existence amounted to a dream of supermasculinity, it thrived on the 'paradox' that the lack and inadequacy which it aimed to abolish were the entailments not merely of traditional femininity but of sexual difference itself. Something more complicated than a conventional chauvinism was involved, which perhaps explains why Marinetti was actually prepared to retract the manifesto's derogatory reference to woman – in the August/September issue of *Poesia* of the same year he commented on

> the terrible nausea we get from the obsession with the ideal woman in works of the imagination, the tyranny of love amongst latin people, and the monotonous *leit-motif* of adultery! A nausea which we have expressed in a perhaps too laconic way by these words: *Scorn for women.*[8]

And in his preface to *Mafarka the Futurist* (1910) Marinetti further emphasized that his real object of attack was 'the sentimental significance' attributed to women.[9] In view of these qualifications, it is a little less surprising to find that the Futurist movement, which we tend to think of as a male-dominated avant-garde *par excellence*, actually included a number of women writers and artists. As Claudia Salaris has shown, the war years saw a lively dialogue about feminism within the movement, and it is clear from some of the writings of the women involved that the *anti-passéisme* of Futurist theory could be appropriated for potentially progressive political positions.[10]

The repudiation of the feminine was, however, more clear-cut at the cultural level: here 'woman' provided the symbolic focus of an attack on those attitudes towards language, subjectivity and sexual difference which now seemed to characterize a Symbolist or decadent poetics (in the early years of the century the two terms became almost interchangeable for purposes of polemic). Marinetti listed 'four intellectual poisons' of decadence:

> 1) the sickly, nostalgic poetry of distance and memory; 2) romantic sentimentality drenched with moonshine that looks up adoringly to the ideal of Woman-Beauty; 3) obsession with lechery, with the adulterous triangle, the pepper of incest, and the spice of Christian sin; 4) the professorial passion for the past and the mania for antiquity and collecting.[11]

This passage brings together a number of major elements: the nineteenth-century tropes of memory and displacement, types of deviant sexuality, excessive sentimentality, and an obsession with the past which leads to academic reclusiveness and fetishism. The female body is the symbolic centre of this set of negative and disabling forces since it is the traditional cultural focus of desire and deferred pleasure, the emblem whose unattainability is conventionally the guarantee of its transcendent power. Note that the emphasis is on the passivity and immobility induced by a romantic fetishism of femininity – not only does the false religion of *amore* effeminize the male (the pale professor in his study), but it also creates a poetics of reflection and solipsism, a hoarding of internal riches against an ever-present sense of lack and incompleteness. Futurism, in contrast, will seek the open spaces of the public domain, abandoning the psychic investment which motivates the symbol (and fetish) in favour of a lavish expenditure worthy of a new consumer age.

Now the immediate lineage of Futurism is fairly clear in this respect: the crop of avant-garde movements which sprang up around the turn of the century – movements we have now largely forgotten, like Naturism, Humanism, Unanism – amounted to a recoil from Symbolism in favour of a more extrovert poetics of collective feeling and social concern. That new emphasis was grounded repeatedly in a call for a new cultural dynamism and virility – 'Poets of today and tomorrow', exhorts one such manifesto, 'let us be men!'[12] In cases like this, the emphasis on masculinity was purely strategic, and generally crudely so, but Marinetti (who in his early years had been closely involved with Symbolism, both as practitioner and translator) picked up on a more complex and less obvious set of connections between language and sexual difference which would inform much subsequent avant-garde thinking. Thus we find him writing in his 1913 manifesto on 'Words-in-Freedom':

> I oppose the decorative, precious aesthetic of Mallarmé and his search for the rare word, the one indispensable, elegant, suggestive, exquisite adjective. I do not want to suggest an idea or a sensation with passéiste airs and graces. Instead I want to grasp them brutally and hurl them in the reader's face.[13]

What Marinetti objects to is Mallarmé's 'static ideal', his fetishistic attention to the single word rather than to 'the beauty of speed' which is the objective of the Futurist 'destruction of syntax'. Of course, Marinetti is perversely inattentive to the rhythmic articulation of Mallarmé's poems, but he has highlighted that aspect of literary style which appealed so strongly to the decadent sensibility. As Huysmans put it in A Rebours, Mallarmé 'avoided dispersing the reader's attention over all the several qualities that a row of adjectives would have presented one by one, concentrating it instead on a single word, a single entity'.[14]

The passage from Mallarmé's Hérodiade which Huysmans's hero, Des Esseintes, so much admires is in this respect a crucial one: Hérodiade is gazing at herself in a mirror and, as she does so, she recognizes for the first time the full force of her own sexual desire. Her triumph, of course, is to deny this desire, and this victory over natural inclination is registered when the mirror too reflects the purity of her resolve:

> ... This mirror that reflects in sleepy calm
> Herodias of diamantine gleam ...
> Yes, final charm! I feel, I am, alone.[15]

The final line perfectly encapsulates that inward turn which the new avant-gardes set out to challenge; but, more importantly, it dramatizes an internalizing of sexual impulse, as unfulfilled desire, which suggests that the denial of natural pleasure and fecundity is rewarded by their reappearance at the level of the signifier. Marinetti's critique of the inertness of Mallarmé's style is rooted in this connection between inhibited sexual impulse and the hermetic depth and materiality of language which seems to be its compensation (the triumph of style over nature). But 'compensation', of course, only in the mirrored world of the decadent imagination, for in Marinetti's terms the closely-worked opacity of Mallarmé's language falsely attracts to itself the allure and corporeality of that eroticized body whose claims it strives to deny. The absorbed inward gaze is, as it were, crystallized in the 'rare word' which becomes a fetishistic object whose material 'weight' inhibits movement and expressivity, confining the imagination to a world of artifice whose law is one of perennially unfulfilled desire. For Marinetti, this is the world of the pre-modern, a world where an economy of accumulation and repression blocks access to any immediate sensual experience of the new. As so often with his thought, Nietzsche lurks in the background; the following passage from *On the Genealogy of Morals* is especially relevant:

All instincts that do not discharge themselves outwardly *turn inward* – this is what I call the *internalization* of man: thus it was that man first developed what was called his 'soul'. The entire inner world, originally as thin as if it were stretched between two membranes, expanded and extended itself, acquired depth, breadth and height in the name of measure as outward discharge was *inhibited*.[16]

Once again we have the theme of a false embodiment or materialization which inhibits the 'outward discharge' which is modernity. The implied analogy between the fulfilment of male desire and the drive of modernization suggests too a parallel tendency to associate a sense of introversion and 'deep' materiality with a notion of femininity. Variously managed, this association would permeate the thought of subsequent Modernist avant-gardes.

If by the turn of the century femininity was felt to have strongly negative cultural associations it was mainly because of that decadent legacy which connected sexual and linguistic excess with social decline and the unsettling of the gender divide (Zola's *La Curée* 1872 provides a relatively early statement of the theme in its presentation of Maxime as 'a strange hermaphrodite making its entrance at the right moment in a society that was growing rotten').[17] Nowhere is this clearer than in an influential polemic by Charles Maurras against what he termed 'feminine romanticism'. Part of the argument of the set of articles Maurras published under this heading in 1903 hinged on an opposition between a masculine classicism and a feminine romanticism which he traced to dubious foreign (i.e. German) origins. More interestingly, Maurras attempted to locate this gender opposition within specific practices of writing. The women writers, he claimed, had at least one thing in common: in their work, 'words acquire material weight, that physical value, that tone, that *carnal pleasure* which must, of necessity, slow down movement, but increase the power of suggestion'.[18] Maurras was seeking a return to 'reason' and the relational economy of classical verse, and in doing so he attacked the familiar modes of symbolist writing – musicality, colour, synaesthesia, even metaphor – as both disruptive of 'signification' and indicative of feminine self-absorption. Marinetti, of course, would have no time for Maurras's *passéisme*, but the contrast drawn here between a 'womanly' preoccupation with the material (especially phonic) properties of language on the one hand, and a virile literature of action on the other, was directly to the point. 'It is', said Maurras, 'a womanly pleasure to handle words like material (*étoffes*). Subtle analogies of sentiment and sensation, poorly discerned or fleetingly conceived by coarse manly intelligences, are here, on the contrary, natural and commonplace elements of the soul's life.'[19]

Given this context, we can see how Futurism's preoccupation with speed and simultaneity derived not simply from an obsession with technology, but from a need to find aesthetic means by which to deny linguistic materiality as the province of a 'feminine' inwardness. In one sense a fundamental paradox was involved here, since the manifestos of Futurism and its programmatic literary texts, like Marinetti's *Zang Tumb Tumb* (1914), promoted 'words-in-freedom' as 'a marvellous bridge between the word and the real thing'[20] and thereby emphasized the value of verbal 'presence' through devices like onomatopoeia. Furthermore, as Marjorie Perloff has argued, Futurism may be seen as having inaugurated a poetic of 'collage', affirming a close tie between verbal and visual which *heightens* the materiality of the signifier.[21] Yet while the Futurist objective of sensory immediacy seems to suggest a closer tie to the linguistic opacity of Symbolism than Marinetti allows, in practice the results are very different and derive from a quite opposite conception of language which we can define provisionally as Modernist. For where the Mallarméan text achieves its effect by an intricate reticulation of surface whose echoes and reflective deferrals project a syntax of desire and dream, the Futurist 'destruction of syntax', with its rejection of 'inevitable echo-play, internal and external',[22] employs juxtaposition and analogy to create a fast-moving surface which denies the Symbolist imagination a foothold. Emotion now tends to be depersonalized: the linear trajectory of the text brutally suppresses any opportunity for introspection, and in place of the structures of syntax Marinetti opts for 'very brief or *anonymous* mathematical and musical symbols'.[23] Movement here is not that of the Symbolist *rêve*, but something apparently external and absolutely enjoined, the movements of 'objects' rather than of the contemplative sensibility: 'To render the successive motions of an object, one must render the *chain of analogies* that it evokes.'[24] In place of the vertical relations presupposed by the symbol (the real as imperfect embodiment of the ideal), the scatter-gun effect of Futurist analogies produces a horizontal cross-weave of images which brings together different, initially unrelated zones of experience. This is, according to Marinetti, writing which banishes both 'materialism' and 'psychology', operating some-where between the two in a kind of hyper-reality where the Nietzschean will-to-power is caught up into the newly liberated forces of the industrial world. The result of this self-transcendence is 'Man multiplied by the machine. New mechanical sense, a fusion of instinct with the efficiency of motors and conquered forces.'[25] This 'fusion' occurs when man is 'able to externalize his will'[26] – the outward force of the will overcomes the 'feminine' tendency to inwardness; hence Marinetti's injunction to 'Destroy the *I* in literature: that is all psychology. . . . To substitute for human psychology, now exhausted, the lyric obsession with matter.'[27]

What we have here is a radical attack on subjectivity as the site of lack and division, and an attempt instead to exteriorize the self by dispersing it within the flow of modern experience. The Futurist project thus aims to dissolve those private intensities of the reflective imagination and eroticized body whose 'feminine' inscriptions (as 'depth' and materiality) offer resistance to the mechanized currents of modernity. The emphasis on flux and movement registers the impact of Bergson's idea of personal time, though here it is as if duration (*duré*) has been 'spatialized', equated with the rhythms of technological and communicational process which mark out the dimensions of the modern life-world.[28] If man is 'multiplied' by the machine it is because his human limitations seem to vanish in a prodigious surrender to the machine which cancels subjectivity at one metaphysical stroke: 'We already live in the absolute, because we have created eternal omnipresent speed.'[29] While the machine embodies a harsh productivist logic, it is one which abolishes the traditional dialectic of private and public, inner and outer, in order to institute a self whose thorough dehumanization is the mark of its triumph over the lack and incompleteness associated with sexual difference:

> We systematically destroy the literary *I* in order to scatter it into the universal vibration and reach the point of expressing the infinitely small and the vibration of molecules. . . . Thus the poetry of cosmic forces supplants the poetry of the merely human.[30]

Marinetti's aim is thus to cancel that association of desire with lack which led Proust, for example, to conclude that 'only the unexpected, that which was never desire's goal, can really make one happy'.[31] Lying behind the Futurist destruction of the *I* is a conception of desire which is strangely close to that which Deleuze and Guattari have more recently proposed:

> Desire does not lack anything; it does not lack its object. It is, rather, the *subject* that is missing in desire, or desire that lacks a fixed subject; there is no fixed subject unless there is repression . . .[32]

This way of connecting desire with reality, liberating the artist from the tyranny of representation and 'the lost Object',[33] transforms the Futurist self into the purely functional conduit of external rhythms. Sexuality is freed from the law of desire to become a purely mechanical genital contact,[34] the body 'metallized' in its transcendence of sexual difference. Desire becomes a kind of 'non-human' force, as Valentine de Saint-Point claims in her *Futurist Manifesto of Lust* (1913): 'Lust, when viewed without moral preconceptions and as an essential part of life's dynamism, is a force.'[35] Futurist theory thus entails a kind of 'decentring': when Marinetti calls for '*strict nets of images or analogies*'[36] the structural model of the net suggests, as Umberto Eco notes in another context, 'no centre, no periphery, no exit, because it is potentially infinite'.[37] No longer a stable centre, subjectivity drains through the holes in the net, denied a 'materialization' in the hermetic word.

Marinetti's attack on the past can, in these terms, be seen as something more extreme than his desire to dynamite museums, repudiating, as it does, one main oppositional thrust of nineteenth-century poetics. For if the development of Symbolism, from Baudelaire on, had been an attempt to open up the divisions in subjectivity in order to call in question bourgeois ideals of rational progress and self-presence, Futurism, in its celebratory dissolution of the self, was really nothing less than an attempt to repair those divisions, to make the subject a transparent vehicle of capitalist modernity.[38] In this sense, the dialectic of destruction and creation on which the transcendence of self and culture depended actually embodied the larger, more devastating logic of capital – a logic which modern theorists were beginning to explain as a necessary relation between ever-increasing productivity and the ensuing competition for markets. So, while the Futurist exaltation of war was hardly idiosyncratic, it exceeded the forms which this took in the work of other avant-gardists. The pre-war passion for violence generally tended to result either from purely nationalist loyalties or from a more confused desire to destroy a conservative and academic culture. Futurism contained both of these elements, but the deeper rationale of its apparently irrational metaphysic was quite simply that of the market.

Not, of course, that Marinetti would have thought of this in such rationalistic terms: for him the circuit of capital was ultimately as inscrutable as the Bergsonian *élan vital* and it was precisely in this measure that it supported a fantasy of modernization as liberating because absolute. As Marinetti put it with his usual bluntness, 'Progress . . . is always right even when it is wrong, because it is movement, life, struggle, hope.'[39] The early preoccupation with speed (Marinetti's 'automobilism') soon yielded to a celebratory sense of the mobility of capital. According to this view, capitalism has no 'logic' as such, but merely articulates a process of never-ending evolution and global expansion. War is 'hygienic' because it encapsulates in the most extreme form the productive and destructive drives within the process of modernization. For Marinetti, it becomes, in the words of one of his critics:

> a *festival* in a psychological sense – as the abolition of norms and as a dispersal of energy –, in a sociological sense – as a magnificent cycle of production and expenditure of goods –, in a political sense – as a pattern of a new order generated from the violent break with the past.[40]

But, as the reference to production and expenditure reminds us, war is the extreme summation of a logic which permeates modernity – the logic of consumerism. This logic the Futurists welcomed as the perfect antidote to a decadent economy of accumulation and repression. Art would no longer be fetishized for its aloofness but would be integrated into the fast-moving circuit of commodities: 'To the conception of the imperishable, the immortal, we oppose, in art, that of becoming, the perishable, the transitory and the ephemeral.'[41] The Futurists may have approached the masses with scorn and cynicism – that after all was the technical discovery of both their manifestos and performances – but they did so in the knowledge that their field of operation was that of the consumer. As one critic observes,

> Art became 'socialized', following not the utopian paths of revolution but rather those of consumption and disposability, an attitude that implies the final disappearance of the 'avant-garde' as value and the advent of a social statute of culture.[42]

If the self was to be thoroughly externalized into the public domain, that was to open it to the manifold stimuli of the market. The world of mass production offered a new range of pleasures; as one Futurist work called *The Death of Woman* (1925) put it: 'Love as sentiment is therefore absurd, an enemy to modern existence where there are no differences between male and female and where the atmosphere is so rich in sensual sensations.'[43] Replacing desire by commodification, Futurism conflated economic expenditure with a celebratory expenditure of the *self* which promised freedom from the limits and incompleteness of a gendered identity.

The full force of this idea is clear when we compare the use of the concept of 'expenditure' in the work of Georges Bataille: for where Bataille affirms waste and expenditure as the transgression of the limits of the purposive world of labour and consumption,[44] Futurism called for an ecstatic and impersonal submission to the homogenizing process of exchange and consumption. So we find Bruno Corradini and Emilio Settimelli in their manifesto of 1914, *Weights, Measures and Prices of Artistic Genius*, insisting that

> The producer of artistic creativity must join the commercial organization which is the muscle of modern life. Money is one of the most formidably and brutally solid points of the reality in which we live. It is enough to turn to it to eliminate all possibility of error and unpunished injustice.[45]

Just as the rapid production of verbal analogies would dissolve subjectivity in its 'net' of images, so money could be grasped as a 'solid point' because it promised the abolition of difference, the perfect metonymic logic in which every element referred inexorably and transparently to the total system.

II

It is this unqualified celebration of modernization which sets Futurism apart from the other main avant-garde movements of the time. Perry

Anderson is, in this respect, wrong to claim that 'In no case was capitalism as such ever exalted by any brand of "modernism" ', though his account of the basis of the general avant-garde interest in the new machine aesthetic does hold good for the other movements: 'The condition of this interest . . . was the abstraction of the techniques and artifacts from the social relations of production that were generating them.'[46] So we find that the various movements tended to condemn the modernolatry of the Futurists, seeking to re-establish a critical distance between culture and capital. The attention to form and design which permeated from Cubism into Vorticism and Purism was a means of subordinating the technological to the aesthetic in such a way as to reinstate the nineteenth-century opposition of art to consumerism. In different ways, these other movements followed the Futurist emphasis on dynamism, often setting up criteria of energy and formal efficiency which were also meant to connote a 'masculine' activism, but the Italian delight in movement as a means of dissolving subjectivity tended to be curbed by a partial return to representation, to an object-based aesthetic. The Cubists, Imagists, and Vorticists were as much preoccupied with 'space' as were the Futurists, but here space was redefined as distance, as a praxis of visual perception which allowed detachment and contemplation rather than immersion in the flows of capital. Ideas of energy and dynamism continued to derive from technology, but outside Futurism they produced models of design and articulation which were valued for the *resistance* they appeared to offer to the movements of exchange and consumption.

This emphasis on articulation – on values of lucidity, clarity, 'objectivity' – was the guarantee at once of psychological unity and of some kind of authentic social horizon (the avant-garde now reoccupying the higher ground)[47] – a guarantee, as it seemed, of resistance to the uncontrollable workings of the unconscious and the chaotic immediacy of the consumer world (the two were frequently bracketed together as purely appetitive orders). As Wyndham Lewis put it, '*Hostility to the word* goes hand in hand with propaganda for the intuitional, mystical chaos.'[48] Lewis's conception of art, like Marinetti's, had no place for romantic interiority, but the ideal aesthetic object proposed by his artist-hero Tarr epitomized a hardness and stasis which evoked the *pre*-Futurist dichotomy between art and life:

> The armoured hide of the hippopotamus, the shell of the tortoise, feathers and machinery, you may put in one camp; naked pulsing and moving of the soft inside of life – along with elasticity of movement and consciousness – that goes in the opposite camp. Deadness is the first condition for art: the second is absence of soul, in the human and sentimental sense. With the statue its lines and masses are its soul, no restless inflammable ego is imagined for its interior: it has *no inside*: good art must have no inside: that is capital.[49]

Lewis's dismissal of the type of art which concerns itself with 'the soft inside of life' is typical of a major tendency within Anglo-American

Modernism. Like Marinetti, Lewis, Pound and Eliot attacked the 'feminine' inwardness and instability of a decadent language, but in doing so they associated its inertness and resistance to the values of the 'masculine' intelligence with that very process of modernization which Futurism had celebrated. For this reason, much of the internal polemic of Anglo-American Modernism purports to decode 'feminine' stylistic traits as the reflection of a self-regarding and degraded culture (Lewis's sustained attacks on the modern culture of 'time' and the unconscious are the monuments to this polemic). Again there is the critique of a 'false' materiality: Eliot, for example, finds in Virginia Woolf's 'feminine type' of writing a failure to externalize feeling, to render it intelligible through objectification;[50] Lewis criticizes the 'heavy, sticky, opaque mass' of Gertrude Stein's language and the 'stupendous outpouring of matter, or stuff' which is Joyce's *Ulysses*;[51] Pound understands historical decline in terms of a loss of clarity, a descent into the 'brown meat' of Rembrandt, the 'thickening' line, and the increasing opacity of the word.[52]

Partly because of the example of Futurism's break with the past and its influential coding of this in gender terms, Modernists like Eliot, Pound, and Lewis were unwilling to look to the language of the unconscious for an oppositional style (in contrast to, say, Stein, Artaud, and the Surrealists).[53] But because their particular Modernism was a *rappel à l'ordre* which (like that of Maurras) depended on a forceful restatement of sexual difference, the feminine 'other' could not be effaced, as it was in the 'cosmic vibrations' of the Futurist world. Indeed, 'feminine' intensities of lack and desire had an important function to serve in, say, the lyric sequences of Pound's *Cantos*, a poem which, at one level, seeks to 'redeem' linguistic materiality through a powerful re-fixing of sexual difference as the precondition – literal and metaphoric – of a just economic order. We must therefore qualify Alan Durant's Lacanian account of Pound's 'desire for the elimination of those aspects of language which reveal the fact of its own plasticity, or of its own material production',[54] an account which hardly does justice to Pound's obvious preoccupation with the phonetic and graphic potentialities of language. We might say instead that Pound attempts to 'repossess' the feminine properties of style – it is not that materiality is repressed, but rather that it is controlled, made the mark of a personal authority through an emphatic lexical and rhythmic discipline (those echoes and recurrent stress patterns which are Pound's 'signature'). Desire thus appears to be stabilized, with the feminine linguistically ordered in relation to the masculine.[55] Exemplary in this respect, *The Cantos* confront the homogenizing space of capital by reinstating those familiar dialectics of subject and object, public and private, past and present, which Futurism had sought to transcend.

III

Not until quite recently, with the theorizing of 'postmodernity', have the extreme perspectives of Futurism been reopened. This is not to propose that Postmodernism is in any sense a 'repeat' of Futurism, but rather that it contains some strikingly similar fantasy elements. 'Fantasy', because they entail various utopian or dystopian ideas of collective destiny which, beginning from an acknowledgement of a general experience of modernization, end by accelerating a surrender to it.

Fredric Jameson's well-known essay on 'Postmodernism, or the cultural logic of late capitalism'[56] is a good place to start. Jameson seeks to define Postmodernism not as a particular body of stylistic developments but as a distinct phase of socio-economic development which, after Ernest Mandel, he calls 'Late Capitalism'. Supplementing the work of Mandel with insights from Jean Baudrillard and others, Jameson characterizes postmodernity as the purest form of capitalism yet to have emerged: in this 'late' stage, capital has colonized the previously sacrosanct areas of nature and the unconscious, incorporating aesthetic production into the general movements of commodity production. The temporal rhythms of an earlier capitalism are now displaced by predominantly spatial forms of figuration. In another essay,[57] Jameson presents this shift in terms of three main phases. Classical or market capitalism had worked on the model of the grid, clarifying space and placing the subject at the centre (its literary mode was realism); with the phase of monopoly capitalism or imperialism, the relation between this structure and individual experience had broken down (producing the discontinuous forms of modernism in the aesthetic sphere); finally, we have the 'hyperspace' of multinational capital, a radically decentred global network whose non-representational forms are those of Postmodernism.

Now all sorts of questions arise from this schema, mainly because of its degree of generality and its projection of Mandel's categories at the phenomenological level of individual experience.[58] What is particularly striking, though, is the reappearance of certain themes from Futurism. To be sure, the 'hyperspace' of postmodernity is seen as alienating rather than emancipatory (though Jameson exhibits a certain ambivalence about this), but we have once again the idea of the subject caught up into a 'total' economic system – and caught up to such a degree that subjectivity is, again, exteriorized in what Jameson calls the 'saturated space' of postmodernity.[59] We witness – for the second time – the disappearance of a whole thematics of 'time and temporality, the elegiac mysteries of *durée* and of memory' (p. 64): 'History' is reduced to pastiche and marketed nostalgia, and aesthetics registers the progressive 'waning of affect', a loss of that depth and temporal reach which hitherto marked the domain of subjectivity. Like Futurism, Postmodernism signals a decline of affectivity, and it is thus not surprising (recalling the earlier repudiation of Symbolist modes) that 'affect' can here return only in the breakdown of the signifying chain. This breakdown – marked now as schizophrenic rather than feminine – produces through the blatant materiality of the signifier 'a mysterious charge of affect' (p. 73), but one which, while it may produce moments of euphoria, is fundamentally disjunct from the contexts of praxis and personal history.

The postmodern subject finds itself adrift in experiential spaces whose magnitude and homogeneity correspond to the 'unmappable' networks of multinational capital. The thematics of speed and instantaneity is fundamental to Jameson's account, but what is most surprising is that the characteristic *closures* of Futurist theory also reappear. The specificities of class, gender and race hardly figure here, and for all his reference to Mandel's systematic theory, Jameson proposes a version of the subject as somehow universalized by the all-penetrating movements of capital. His description of the Bonaventura Hotel is a case in point – here the subject (any subject) is caught up in an experience of the 'hysterical sublime' which registers 'the limits of figuration and the incapacity of the human mind to give representation to such enormous forces' (p. 77). Fantasy or lived reality? Jameson's concern seems to be with the detail of perceptual experience, but the universalizing of this sense of homelessness and disorientation almost makes us forget that experiences such as these are often ones which powerfully reopen questions of individual status and power. The same objection can be levelled at the other model so favoured by postmodernist theory, that of the subject as consumer: once again, the subject is made to disappear at precisely those moments when the matter of *difference* between individuals is so palpably present.[60]

How does Jameson arrive at this position? It is partly a result of his attempt to think Postmodernism dialectically, as both positive and negative, as Simon During has argued. During observes that, for Jameson, the internationalism of postmodernity promises the eradication of post-colonial nationalisms. This view of Postmodernism conceals, however, an ideology of progress, and During notes that 'one can be forgiven for thinking that Jameson is harnessing all the power inherent in images of totalitarianism to eradicate cultural difference in the old spirit of enlightened modernity'.[61] Of course, we know that this isn't what Jameson really wants, but the blurring of differences, sexual as well as ethnic, is the unexpected product of the powerful pull of the postmodern fantasy. As with Futurism, these images of decentred networks and 'absolute' process are powered by a sense of extremity and hyperbole which here situates them in an equivocal space somewhere between utopia and dystopia. Needless to say, this is all a far cry from *Late Capitalism*, Jameson's starting-point. For whatever the merits of Mandel's analysis, his book gives (as we might expect from a Marxist economist) a strong sense of the contradictory processes at work within modern capitalism. Such processes are, for Mandel, perfectly 'mappable', and their distinguishing features derive precisely from 'the *lack of homo-geneity* of the capitalist world economy' which is a product of 'the constant combination of development and underdevelopment'.[62] In contrast to Jameson's view of the subject helplessly adrift in hyperspace,

Mandel's analysis signals points of resistance and incoherence within the economy – resistance, that is, which may be 'a necessary outcome of the unfolding laws of motion of capitalism itself' (p. 85) or a product of a more clearly activist and global 'process of contestation' (p. 586) which develops from a crisis within the relations of production.

If Jameson's references to Mandel's theory of late capitalism seem uneasy components of his concept of postmodernity, other more deliberately post-Marxist versions of the theme are less troubled with ambiguities. For such theories, postmodernity registers the passing of a society which can be understood in terms of industrial production and class conflict. The contemporary world is here imagined as one in which use value and personal needs have been overwhelmed by the circulation of exchange values – the individual is dispersed into a network of circulating signs whose only referent is the totality of the system itself. For Jean Baudrillard, the best-known exponent of such theories, commodities are no longer material objects but rather 'social signifiers', part of a 'code' for which the medium is truly the message. Individuals are 'only episodic conductors of meaning' in a system in which 'there are only needs because the system needs them'.[63] Baudrillard's theory is, once again, premised on the transcendence of desire and difference, as is clear from his well-known essay on 'The ecstasy of communication'. Like most postmodern theory, Baudrillard's essay assumes the disappearance of the old avant-gardist position but it none the less repeats the earlier myth of modernity as absolute rupture. There was previously, says Baudrillard,

a domestic scene, a scene of interiority, a private space-time (correlative, moreover, to a public space). The oppositions subject/object and public/private were still meaningful. . . . But today the scene and mirror no longer exist; instead, there is a screen and a network. In place of the reflexive transcendence of mirror and scene, there is a nonreflecting surface where operations unfold – the smooth operational surface of communication.[64]

This network of communication is conceived in now familiar terms, as a spatializing of those psychic areas which were once private and temporal:

what was projected psychologically and mentally, what used to be lived out on earth as metaphor, as mental and metaphorical scene, is henceforth projected into reality, without any metaphor at all, into an absolute space which is also that of simulation.[65]

The 'ecstasy of communication' is a condition in which 'All secrets, spaces and scenes [are] abolished in a single dimension of information.'[66] Baudrillard concludes with the observation that 'in any case, we will have to suffer this new state of things, this forced extroversion of all interiority, this forced injection [sic] of all interiority that the categorical imperative of communication literally signifies.'[67] While the Futurist elision of inner and outer had produced ecstatic liberation, the postmodern condition places us in a state of terror proper to the schizophrenic: too great a proximity of everything, the unclean promiscuity of everything which touches, invests and penetrates without resistance, with no halo of private protection. . . . It is the end of interiority and intimacy, the over-exposure and transparence of the world which traverses [the subject] without obstacle.

Whatever we think of Baudrillard's argument – and it is one which, as Mark Poster has said, 'accepts too easily the omnipotence of the semiological structure'[68] – its underlying perspective is still a critical one. With the publication in 1986 of *Amérique*, however, the postmodern fantasy emerges full-blown. Like other recent French theorists, Baudrillard seizes on America as the very image of postmodernity, a gesture which recalls, of course, the early Modernist infatuation with the 'Cubist, the Futurist' city of New York, as Picabia described it.[69] But where the interest of Picabia and Duchamp had been a partially ironic one, focusing mainly on potentialities of design, Baudrillard's way of contrasting America with Europe recalls the Futurist Boccioni's expression of 'the need to Americanise ourselves, to enter into the overwhelming vortex of modernity'.[70] For what America is seen to offer here is not a repertoire of innovative forms, but a sensory experience which is governed once more by speed and simultaneity. The central image of *Amérique* is that of the desert, or rather of driving through the desert at speed. The experience is one in which all reference points disappear in pure 'horizontality': the sense of time is lost, as the speed of driving coincides with a landscape whose timeless geology merges with the unthinkable technological power of the atomic test.[71] Speed, says Baudrillard, is 'the triumph of instantaneity over time as depth, the triumph of the surface and of pure objectness [*objectalité*] over the depth of desire' (p. 20). Driving through the silent spaces of the desert is like the 'pure circulation' (p. 55) of the economic world: it is a mark of the 'realised utopia' (p. 194) which is America, a liberation from 'melancholy European analyses' into a freedom which is now a condition not of the inner self but of the subject as consumer: 'freed is the man who changes spaces, who circulates, who changes sex, clothes, manners according to fashion, *and not according to morality*' (p. 192). This is the lesson of speed which, like the freeway, its privileged space, gives access to a communal experience stripped of the affectivity of individual desires. Not, of course, that there is any sociality here, only a 'collective compulsion', a 'functional participation' (p. 107) which saves us from individual existence and 'responsibility'. This is the ultimate fantasy of decentring, for the instantaneity of America both dissolves the self and makes it reappear as part of a centre which is everywhere – the smallest suburb, says Baudrillard, encapsulates America, being 'closer to the centre of the world than any cultural manifestation of old Europe' (p. 56).

Remarks such as this remind us that this particular postmodern experience, with its loss of the referent, is very much the limited experience of the tourist. Is there now a Postmodernist Grand Tour, an itinerary of America which provides this view of its culture rather than any other (Hollywood rather than Watts)? Perhaps there is, because we find Baudrillard also making the obligatory visit to the Bonaventura Hotel. Here, once again, this 'illusionist architecture' registers the loss of interface between interior and exterior (p. 118) marking that 'violent extroversion' (p. 151) which lies at the heart of this apocalyptic fantasy. For Baudrillard, much as for Marinetti and the Futurists, such experiences point toward a final destruction of differences. And if Marinetti's 'machine-man' now seems both ridiculous and repellent, that figure seems to reappear in Baudrillard's evocation of 'this orgy of liberation, this orgy of indifference, of disconnection, of exhibition and circulation' (p. 192). The 'orgy' is, as we might now expect, one which announces the 'end' of sexuality. In America, sexuality has yielded to 'gender', a sign-system of visual appearances rather than a pattern of drives and desires. The 'indifference' of American culture is tantamount to 'the recession of sexual characteristics' (p. 94):

> Ultimately, there would no longer be masculine and feminine, but a dissemination of separate sexes referring only to themselves, each one managing itself as a separate enterprise. End of seduction, end of difference, and a slide toward another system of values. (p. 95)

While postmodernity is awash with sexual images, the world of 'pure circulation' no longer allows sexuality 'the time to materialize in human love relationships, it evaporates in constant promiscuity, in the most ephemeral multiple contacts' (p. 49).

That quotation brings my argument full circle, making the connection yet again between materiality and sexual difference – a connection which Baudrillard, like the Futurists before him, seeks to dissolve in the dizzying and abstract spaces of modernization. And these spaces are abstract in several senses, for their 'sublimity' brings not only (in Baudrillard's phrase) the 'end of the social', but also, to retain his idiom, an end of language as a social means. Just as the Futurists sought the destruction of syntax, putting in its place an abstract grammar of functional mathematical signs, so America seems to offer the example of a culture which is 'space, speed, cinema, technology'.[72] Baudrillard's rather lame conclusion, that in America 'life is cinema' (p. 201), signals an apocalyptic elision of culture and technology which announces the 'end' of the speaking subject. The idea that, as he puts it in *In the Shadow of the Silent Majorities*, 'a system is abolished only by pushing it into hyperlogic'[73] seems, finally, less a ground of possible negation than – like Futurism – a delirious surrender to forces which must always lie beyond control and understanding. The fantasy is, like the image, all that we have – or rather, all that such theories allow us to have; for if the comparison with Futurism has a purpose it is surely to remind us that these *are* fantasies and not unspeakable necessities.

University of Sussex

An earlier version of this paper was presented to the Bruce Centre, University of Keele. I am grateful to Alistair Davies, Paul Edwards, and Richard Godden for their advice on revision. Unless otherwise indicated, all translations are my own.

1 Wyndham Lewis, 'The melodrama of modernity', *Blast*, 1 (June 20, 1914), p. 143; Ezra Pound, 'Vorticism' (1914), rpt. *Gaudier Brzeska* (1916; Hessle: Marvell Press, 1960), p. 82. On the reception of Futurism in England, see especially Giovanni Cianci, 'Futurism and the English avant-garde: the early Pound between Imagism and Vorticism', *Arbeiten aus Anglistik und Amerikanistik*, 1 (1981), pp. 3–39.

2 Marjorie Perloff, *The Futurist Moment: Avant-garde, Avant-guerre, and the Language of Rupture* (Chicago and London: University of Chicago Press, 1986), p. 195, argues that contemporary performance art, visual poetry, and intermedia works amount to 'what we might call a disillusioned or cool Futurism'. Perloff explores the connection through the concept of collage, a formal emphasis which differs from that of the present essay. See also my 'Machines and collages', *Journal of American Studies*, 22, 2 (August 1988), pp. 275–80.

3 *The Founding and Manifesto of Futurism* (1909), tr. in R. W. Flint (ed.), *Marinetti: Selected Writings* (London: Secker & Warburg, 1972), p. 41 (hereafter cited as Flint).

4 ibid., p. 42. See also the discussion in Rosalind E. Krauss, *The Originality of the Avant-garde and Other Modernist Myths* (Cambridge, Mass. and London: MIT Press, 1987), p. 157.

5 Flint, p. 42.

6 *Futurist Democracy* (1919), Flint, p. 77.

7 Flint, p. 91.

8 Quoted in Claudia Salaris, *Le futuriste: Donne e letteratura d'avanguardia in Italia (1909/1944)* (Milan: Edizioni delle donne, 1982), p. 23. This anthology is the principal source for information on women and Futurism, though Salaris's *Storia del Futurismo* (Rome: Editori Riuniti, 1985) is also helpful. Mina Loy's 'Aphorisms on Futurism', in Roger L. Conover (ed.), *The Last Lunar Baedeker* (Highlands, NC: Jargon Society, 1982), pp. 272–5, provides an interesting comparison.

9 ' "Mafarka il futurista": Prefazione', in Luciano De Maria (ed.), *Opere di F. T. Marinetti*, vol. 2: *Teoria e invenzione futurista* (Milan: Mondadori, 1968), p. 217.

10 Claudia Salaris's anthology indicates two main centres of activity for these women writers: the Florentine review *L'Italia futurista* (1916–18) and *Roma futurista* (1918–20). Contributions to the former include a number of interesting reponses to Marinetti's *Come si seducono le donne* (1917) – see particularly those of Enif Robert, Rosa Rosà, and Shara Marini. Interventions in *Roma futurista* indicate feminist initiatives within the Futurist Political Party (1918–20).

11 *War, the World's Only Hygiene* (1911–15), Flint, p. 68.

12 Fernand Gregh, 'Manifeste humaniste' (1902), rpt. in Bonner Mitchell (ed.), *Les Manifestes littéraires de la belle époque* (Paris: Seghers, 1966), p. 74. This collection usefully reprints most of the main manifestos of the period.

13 *Destruction of Syntax – Imagination without Strings – Words-in-Freedom*

(1913), tr. in Umbro Apollonio (ed.), *Futurist Manifestoes*, tr. Robert Brain *et al.* (New York: Viking Press, 1973), p. 105 (hereafter cited as Apollonio).

14 Joris-Karl Huysmans, *Against Nature*, tr. Robert Baldick (Harmondsworth: Penguin Books, 1959), pp. 196–7.

15 *Mallarmé: The Poems*, tr. Keith Bosley (Harmondsworth: Penguin Books, 1977), p. 113.

16 Friedrich Nietzsche, *On the Genealogy of Morals*, tr. Walter Kaufmann (New York: Vintage Books, 1969), p. 184.

17 *La Curée: The Kill*, tr. A. Teixeira de Mattos (London: Panther Books, 1985), p. 109.

18 Charles Maurras, *L'Avenir de l'intelligence* (1905; Paris: Flamarion, 1927), p. 212.

19 ibid., p. 214.

20 *La cinematografia futurista* (1916), in *Teoria e invenzione futurista*, p. 120.

21 Perloff, *The Futurist Moment*, p. 191

22 *Destruction of Syntax* (1913), Apollonio, p. 99.

23 ibid., p. 104 (my italics).

24 *Technical Manifesto of Futurist Literature* (1912), Flint, p. 86.

25 *Destruction of Syntax*, Apollonio, p. 97.

26 *War, the World's Only Hygiene* (1911–15), Flint, p. 91.

27 *Technical Manifesto of Futurist Literature*, Flint, p. 87. Luciano De Maria, *Teoria e invenzione futurista*, pp. xlviii-xlix, observes that 'matter' for Marinetti, as for Bergson, is 'an ensemble of images'.

28 The main idea which the Futurists drew from Bergson was that of the indivisibility of movement, as noted in Umberto Boccioni, *The Plastic Foundations of Futurist Sculpture and Painting* (1913), Apollonio, p. 89. The Futurists ignored the role of memory in Bergson's theory of perception, just as they passed over his rejection of instantaneity.

29 *The Founding and Manifesto of Futurism*, Flint, p. 41.

30 *Geometric and mechanical splendor and the numerical sensibility* (1914), Flint, p. 98.

31 Quoted in Peter Szondi, *Theory of the Modern Drama*, tr. M. Hays (Cambridge: Polity Press, 1987), p. 88.

32 Gilles Deleuze and Félix Guattari, *Anti-Oedipus: Capitalism and Schizophrenia*, tr. Robert Hurley *et al.* (London: Athlone Press, 1984), p. 26.

33 Giacomo Balla and Fortunato Depero, *Futurist Reconstruction of the Universe* (1915), Apollonio, p. 198: 'The hands of the traditionalist artist ached for the lost Object . . .'.

34 See Marinetti, *War, the World's Only Hygiene*, Flint, p. 73, and Giovanni Lista (ed.), *Marinetti et le Futurisme* (Lausanne: L'Age d'Homme, 1977), pp. 85–6.

35 Apollonio, p. 70. Cf. Deleuze and Guattari, *Anti-Oedipus*, p. 294: 'Desiring-machines are the non-human sex . . .'.

36 *Technical Manifesto of Futurist Literature*, Flint, p. 86.

37 Umberto Eco, *Reflections on the name of the Rose* (London: Secker & Warburg, 1985), p. 57.

38 According to Valentine de Saint-Point's redefinition, the force of lust and desire 'drives the great men of business who direct the banks . . .' (Apollonio, p. 71).

39 *War, the World's Only Hygiene*, Flint, p. 82.

40 Mario Isnenghi, *Il Mito della Grande Guerra da Marinetti a Malaparte* (Bari:

Laterza, 1970), p. 170. Cf. Eduardo Sanguinetti, 'La Guerre Futuriste', tr. Marcel Oddon in Lista (ed.), *Marinetti et le Futurisme*, pp. 107–11.

41 *War, the World's Only Hygiene*, Flint, p. 67.

42 Germano Celant, 'Futurism as Mass Avant-garde', in Anne D'Harnoncourt (ed.), *Futurism and the International Avant-garde* (Philadelphia: Philadelphia Museum of Art, 1980–1), p. 39.

43 Luigi Colombo Fillia, *La morte della donna* (1925), quoted in Roberto Tessari, *Il mito della macchina: letteratura e industria nel primo novecento* (Milan: Mursia, 1973), p. 258.

44 Georges Bataille, *Visions of Excess: Selected Writings, 1927–39*, tr. Allan Stoekl *et al.* (Manchester: Manchester University Press, 1985), pp. 116–29. See also the discussion of Bataille in Jürgen Habermas, *The Philosophical Discourse of Modernity*, tr. Frederick Lawrence (Cambridge, Mass.: MIT Press, 1987).

45 Apollonio, p. 149.

46 Perry Anderson, 'Modernity and revolution', *New Left Review*, 144 (March–April 1984), p. 105.

47 See, for example, Wyndham Lewis, *Time and Western Man* (London: Chatto & Windus, 1927), p. 5: 'For our only terra firma in a boiling and shifting world is, after all, our "self". That must cohere for us to be capable at all of behaving in any way but as mirror-images of alien realities, or as the most helpless and lowest organisms, as worms or as sponges.'

48 ibid., p. 352.

49 *Tarr* (second version) (1928; London: Calder & Boyers, 1968), pp. 279–80.

50 T. S. Eliot, 'London letter', *Dial*, 71 (August 1921), pp. 216–17: Woolf's writing 'makes its art by feeling, and by contemplating the feeling rather than the object which has excited it, or into which the feeling might be made'. See the discussion of Eliot's habit of ascribing a 'pathology' to this type of writing in Andrew Ross, *The Failure of Modernism* (New York: Columbia University Press, 1986).

51 *Time and Western Man*, pp. 77, 108.

52 See Cantos LXXX and XLV for example, in *The Cantos of Ezra Pound* (London: Faber & Faber, 1975), pp. 511, 229.

53 Recent work on Stein, H. D., Mina Loy and others has begun to propose an alternative, female Modernism which might be seen to reappropriate that materiality effaced or curtailed in the mainstream Anglo-American version. See, for example, Shari Benstock, *Women of the Left Bank: Paris 1900–40* (London: Virago Press, 1986).

54 Alan Durant, *Ezra Pound: Identity in Crisis* (Brighton: Harvester, 1981), p. 22.

55 In *The Cantos*, money is ultimately associated with 'bad' materiality, with imprecision and deviance; see my *Ezra Pound: Politics, Economics and Writing* (London: Macmillan, 1984).

56 *New Left Review*, 146 (July–August 1984), pp. 53–92. Further page references will be given in the text.

57 Fredric Jameson, 'Cognitive mapping', in Cary Nelson and Lawrence Grossberg (eds), *Marxism and the Interpretation of Culture* (Basingstoke: Macmillan, 1988), pp. 349–50.

58 For more empirical objections, see Mike Davis, 'Urban renaissance and the spirit of postmodernism', *New Left Review*, 151 (May–June 1985), pp. 106–13.

59 'Cognitive mapping', p. 351.

60 Cf. Terry Eagleton, 'Capitalism, modernism and post-modernism', *New Left Review*, 152 (July–August 1985), pp. 71–2.

61 Simon During, 'Postmodernism or post-colonialism today', *Textual Practice*, 1, 1 (Spring 1987), p. 35.

62 Ernest Mandel, *Late Capitalism* (London: New Left Books, 1975), pp. 84, 85. Further references will be given in the text.

63 *In the Shadow of the Silent Majorities* (New York: Semiotext(e), 1983), p. 11; *For a Critique of the Political Economy of the Sign* (St Louis: Telos Press, 1981), p. 82.

64 'The ecstasy of communication', in Hal Foster (ed.), *Postmodern Culture* (London and Sydney: Pluto Press, 1985), pp. 126–7. The essay is excerpted from Jean Baudrillard's *Les Stratégies fatales* (Paris: Grasset, 1983).

65 ibid., p. 128. Cf. the quotation from Deleuze and Guattari, p. 208 above.

66 ibid., p. 131. 'Ecstasy', one assumes, is used here with its original Greek meaning, as 'a standing outside oneself'.

67 ibid., p. 132.

68 Mark Poster, 'Technology and culture in Habermas and Baudrillard', *Contemporary Culture*, 22, 4 (Fall 1981), p. 476.

69 Quoted in A. F. Wertheim, *The New York Little Renaissance* (New York: New York University Press, 1976), p. 207.

70 Quoted in Richard Cork, *Vorticism and Abstract Art in the First Machine Age*, 2 vols (London: Fraser, 1976), I, 255.

71 Jean Baudrillard, *Amérique* (Paris: Grasset, 1986), pp. 15–16. Further references will be given in the text. A translation is soon to be published by Verso.

72 Cf. Julia Kristeva on the strength of a 'non-verbal' culture in America, in 'Why the United States?', tr. Seán Hand, in Toril Moi (ed.), *The Kristeva Reader* (Oxford: Basil Blackwell, 1986), pp. 275–6.

73 *In the Shadow of the Silent Majorities*, p. 46.

LISA MOORE

Sexual agency in Manet's Olympia

As a feminist critic, I find Manet's 1863 *Olympia* a dangerous temptation. There are many conduits for reading the image as a strong and subversive one: the direct gaze of the reclining woman is so different from the coy glance of the traditional nude; her nakedness is so clearly a temporary state of being unclothed rather than a 'natural' one of permanent sexual availability; and the contemporary interior she inhabits is not the mythologized boudoir, unknown to history, in which the nude usually resides. All these details support the contention that Manet's image is that of a 'real' woman who controls access to her sexuality rather than a passive object of male fantasy.[1] I am tempted, then, to celebrate for once; such depictions are rare in the canon of art history. I am figuring this reading as a temptation, however, because behind my enjoyment of Olympia's directness, her sauciness, her concreteness, is the cautionary knowledge that this image *is* an important part of the canon. It is a monument in the history of the nude, the very convention I am hoping it unseats. Can *Olympia* be the site of a feminist critique of representation, or does its relation to the institutions of art history and the avant-garde disable its subversive potential?

In order to answer this question, I wish to examine the problem of agency in the painting. One of the major reasons for the painting's hostile reception at the 1865 Salon, I will argue, is that its formal innovations work against the convention of the nude, a convention whose main effect in art history has been to confirm the authority of the male viewer. (In 1860s Paris, of course, this viewer was also bourgeois and white.) Although many formal elements contribute to this unsettling of bourgeois white male subjectivity, the structure of the gaze in the painting is perhaps the most crucial. Drawing on feminist visual analysis and film theory, I will suggest that the painting forestalls the viewer's traditional role as the initiator of meaning, desire and consumption with regard to the work, and endows the figures of the women – Olympia herself and the black maidservant – with that agency. The painting, then, unsettles a whole series of artistic and social conventions.

Such questions as ideology, representation, and institutional critique are addressed by T. J. Clark in his 1985 book, *The Painting of Modern Life: Paris in the Art of Manet and his Followers*. The book has attracted well-deserved attention from theorists in other fields as well as from art

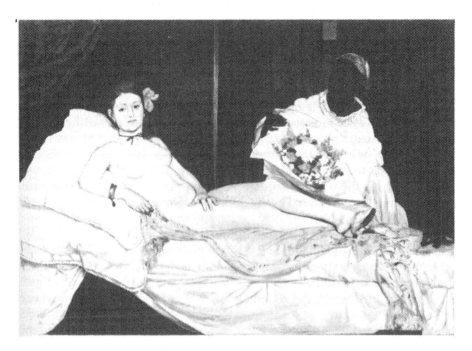

Edouard Manet, *Olympia*, 1863. Paris: Musée d'Orsay. Cliché des Musées Nationaux, Paris.

historians. Clark's is a thoroughly researched and persuasive analysis of the emergence of modern subjectivity in late nineteenth-century Paris as it was inflected by early modernist painting. 'Olympia's choice', his chapter on Manet's *Olympia*, is the fullest and most nuanced reading I have seen of the political implications of the painting's iconoclasm. Speaking of the painting's 1865 viewers, Clark argues that 'the critics' sneering claim not to be able to see or describe *Olympia*' is due to the way in which the painting instantiates class in the prostitute's body, showing that money was 'inflecting everything . . . even those corners of life the culture wished to have private and "personal".'[2] Clark's is a suggestive account of why nineteenth-century critics could not look at *Olympia*; my own analysis will reveal that Clark's vision too is obstructed.

The most interesting aspects of Clark's chapter focus on the historically determined signification of the body of the courtesan. Clark argues that this body, rather than that of the conventionally ahistorical nude, is what was represented and recognized in *Olympia*, posing a disturbing threat to the bourgeois viewer by raising the possibility that 'the body and money would not be unmediated terms any longer, intersecting in the abstract, out there in the hinterland of images; they would take their place as determinate facts in a particular class formation'.[3] What Clark does not quite see here, however, is that class is only part of the story: ultimately, it is Olympia's sexual agency that determines this painting's effect on its bourgeois viewers.[4]

Clark does explicitly raise the question of sexuality, of course. By giving the female body a specific sexual valence, Clark claims, Manet's painting contradicts the assertion of the traditional nude that there is no such thing as female sexuality. In the nude, '*nothing* is what has to be hidden, and indicated by other conventions'.[5] In other words, as psychoanalysis tells us, the female genitals are not represented – because there is nothing there to represent – but then this very lack is so horrible that it cannot be represented either. Whether depicted as a formless blank or covered with a demure hand or wrap, the nude's pubic area must deflect rather than attract attention. This realization explains the otherwise inexplicable scandal over the depiction of Olympia's left hand: the sign for absence doesn't disappear here, as the wrap of Ingres's *Venus Anadyomène* does, but is, as Clark describes it, 'tensed, hard-edged and definite, not an absence, not a thing which yields or includes and need not be noticed'.[6] Similarly, the treatment of Olympia's hair was shocking. Long flowing tresses are of course a very conventional way to indicate female sexiness: such hair, Clark says, 'is a strong sign and a safe one . . . since hair on the head can be combed out and pinned up again in due course'.[7] Most viewers assume that Olympia's hair is pulled back out of sight, thus contributing to her 'manishness', but Clark points out that there *is* a froth of red-brown hair spilling out beneath the red flower. It is just hard to see because of the red-brown screen directly behind it. Olympia seems to have two faces: the hard-edged, businesslike, hairless one, and the much more easily recognizable 'feminine' one framed by the fall of hair. 'Neither face is ever quite suppressed by the other, nor can they be made into aspects of the same image, the same imaginary whole.'[8] Orders of signs thus interfere with one another in this painting, disrupting the function of the nude as a comforting, appropriate containment of three-dimensional reality. In its conscious refutation of this function, Clark argues, Manet's *Olympia* is an attempt to call into question what and how we see.

In the process of this analysis, however, Clark himself has managed not to see the painting itself – not all of it, at least. Because for him the subject is always ultimately a *class* subject, his insights about sexuality remain subordinate to his discussion of economic relations in 1860s Paris. Thus, although he ostensibly argues that it is the *intersection* of class and sexuality that constitutes *Olympia*'s threat, this pairing is not finally a dialectic, but a hierarchy. Clark's analysis prevents him from exploring representations of sexuality in the painting in any systematic fashion. This constraint, in turn, forces him to overlook what is actually there on the canvas. In his discussion of the 'figure' in the painting, he repeatedly assumes that there is only one. The black woman standing practically in the centre of the canvas is consistently overlooked. Such an omission would be serious in any case, but it is especially perilous for Clark's argument because the presence of the black woman is the canvas's most important sexual and class marker. First of all, she literally brings sex into the image in the act of offering the lover's flowers. Sander Gilman has pointed out that in the nineteenth century the representation of black women was a veritable artistic convention for uncontainable sexuality – precisely the quality Clark argues for in *Olympia*. And her presence helps determine Olympia's class, which Clark insists on. Certainly Olympia may be a *petite foubourienne* but she is not a slave. In fact, she is served by one. Formally, the shadowy outlines of the black woman's face and her tendency to be absorbed into the black background establish the clearly outlined white figure's materiality: while in some ways that materiality may be, as Clark argues, undecidable, it situates the figure far more clearly than that of the ever-vanishing black woman. Her presence as a convention seems to be in constant antagonism to her presence as a figure (a subject) in the painting, rendering her both highly visible (in the centre of the painting, holding bright flowers) and difficult to see (her face constantly threatening to disappear into the dark background). In fact, the black figure is the most unrepresented and unrepresentable element in the painting: surely Clark's thesis, that modernity precisely consists in seeing the unrepresentable – in the case of *Olympia*, the intersection of sex and money – should account for her presence.

In my own reading of *Olympia*, then, I would like both to fill in some of the gaps in Clark's suggestive account, and to challenge his categories of analysis from the vantage point of that school of feminist visual analysis which expands on Lacanian psychoanalysis.[9] Perhaps, then, it is appropriate to begin my examination of *Olympia* by trying to account for a troubling element that this painting shares with that other notorious canvas of 1863, *Déjeuner sur l'herbe*: the depiction of a direct feminine gaze from the nude to the viewer. Michael Fried points out that

> there is not a single large multi-figure painting in Manet's *œuvre* in which more than one of those figures looks out at us. . . . I believe that Manet seems consciously or otherwise to have felt that to have *more* than a single figure look directly at the beholder would in effect be to establish a number of individual, and so to speak merely psychological, relationships between the beholder on one hand and the figures in question on the other. Whereas Manet seems to have wanted to establish a particular kind of relationship between the beholder and the painting as a *whole*, in its essential unity as a *painting*. In this sense it is as though the *painting itself* looks or gazes or stares at one – it is as though it confronts, fixes, even *freezes* one.[10]

The utility of this observation for me is that it raises the problem of agency: who is responsible for 'activating' the painting, for making it part of the world? Traditionally, critics, painters, and viewers alike have assumed that the viewer, through his or her gaze, creates meaning for the painting. In the act of seeing, the viewer connects the image with his or her physical reality, whether the painting makes possible recognition, comparison, or challenge with respect to that reality. The role of the image is to enable the viewer to see the world in a slightly different or illuminating way, but the painting cannot initiate this process. Thus, devices such as perspective, foreshortening, chiaroscuro, and modelling had been viewed since the Renaissance as attempts to make the painted image more and more 'real', more and more like what the viewer saw on either side of the frame. The painter's goal, in this limited sense, was thus to accommodate the viewer who would in turn, through the gaze, allow the painting to become meaningful. But as Fried's comment indicates, the direct stares of the nudes in *Olympia* and the *Déjeuner* challenge the male viewer's agency and authority – they '*freeze*' rather than empower him. As Clark notes, these stares are recognizing and recognizable: they look at the French viewer of 1863 from a familiar environment, with a familiar expression, and presume familiarity with the viewer. In fact, it is the extreme verisimilitude of these paintings that seems to be the problem: Olympia is gazing from her couch in a brothel at a viewer who knows from that grimy, familiar couch itself that it is a brothel – and this knowledge implicates him in the sordid scene.

What Fried's comment elides, however, is the significance of this confrontational gaze as part of the image of a woman – specifically, a nude. As I have argued, the traditional purpose of the nude was precisely *not* to challenge the male viewer's agency. Feminist analysis of the gaze in film theory suggests that, by convention, the meaningful gaze is definitively male. According to Ann Kaplan, 'men do not simply look; their gaze carries with it the power of action and possession that is lacking in the female gaze. Women receive and return a gaze, but cannot act on it.'[11] To conceive of Kaplan's structure in terms of the present argument: the only gaze, and the only desire, possible in a picture such as Ingres's *Venus Anadyomène* is that of the male viewer. He activates the sexual content of the picture through his gaze (which of course enters the image through stand-ins such as the putti), thus making the nude sexual because it enables the male viewer to experience sexual feelings. Laura Mulvey distinguishes between two modes of representation made possible by the gaze: a mode in which the male viewer looks directly at the representation of a fetishized female body from which he gains erotic pleasure, and another mode in which the viewer gains pleasure through identification with a male viewer within the frame (a stand-in figure such as Ingres's putti). In both cases, it is clear that the represented woman is not sexual because she herself exudes or exemplifies or enacts her own desire, but because there exist in the painting conventions, including that of a naked female body, through which (male) desire can be enacted.

Agency, then, is linked to the male gaze by formal convention or genre. It is not readily transferable from the male viewer (subject) to the female image (object). What, then, are we to make of the defiant stares of Manet's nudes, which Clark claims indicate a feminine desire that the represented woman produces and owns? Fried points to *Olympia* as 'the closest thing to an exception' to his rule cited above, a painting 'in which both Victorine Meurend [the model who posed as Olympia] and the black cat at the foot of her bed confront us directly'.[12] Perhaps what troubles Fried, as it does Clark, and as it did the bourgeois white male viewers of 1865, is the presence of the third gaze in the painting: that of the black maidservant. The position of her gaze at the apex of this triangle of gazes gives hers a striking formal prominence. This prominence is all the more remarkable when we consider the tendency of viewers not to see this image because of its content: that of a black woman, doubly marginal and hence doubly invisible. Of course, her gaze does not confront the viewer, but rather points at the nude: the black woman here takes on the role attributed to putti or dolphins in traditional nude representations, that of the stand-in for the male viewer and the formal device that allows his desire to be enacted in gazing at the image.

There is, of course, a substantial difference between a chubby little boy angel as an enabling device for male desire and a black woman as the same device. Mulvey's account of the structure of the gaze depends upon the identification of the male viewer with another male figure within the representation. A female figure cannot perform this function, for its efficacy depends upon 'the spectator fascinated with the image of his like . . . and through him gaining control and possession of the woman'.[13] If the category of gender renders the black woman's position in the painting incoherent, so does the category of race. Gilman's work on nineteenth-century sexual and racial iconography makes it clear that the black woman was an overdetermined sexual signifier for the age: her ability to bring sexuality into the painting, as he argues she does,[14] depends on a social tradition that invests the formal marker with a content that threatens to undermine that very function. The black woman for nineteenth-century Europe represented the ultimate form of threatening female desire. She was associated with deviance, physical deformity, illness, and bestiality, as well as excessive sexuality. Gilman notes that 'one of the central functions of the black servant in the visual arts of the eighteenth and nineteenth centuries was as a marker of the sexualization of the society in which he or she was found.'[15] The piquancy of the black figure would have been conventionally used as a marker of sexual mystery and otherness, much as the Oriental surroundings operate in Ingres's or Delacroix's exotic interiors. In these paintings, the racial is completely drained of specificity and becomes a sexual marker no different from the phallic opium pipe in Delacroix's *Femmes d'Algiers*. But the active gaze of the black woman in the painting invokes this tradition in a way that seriously complicates her 'stand-in' function. The difference between a black woman in *Olympia* and in other nineteenth-century paintings is that here she is a conduit, not just a marker. She has to have some kind of agency, even if it is formal or fictional, in order to facilitate the male gaze. The fringe of the bedspread, for instance, signifies sexuality in the painting through its allusion to Olympia's pubic hair, but it need not have agency to do this. The black woman, then, gains her agency from the

Jean-Auguste Dominique Ingres,
Venus Anadyomène, 1848.
Chantilly, Musée Condé.
Photographie Giraudon.

interaction of racist stereotypes of her libidinousness (which give her a sexual function) *and* her formal conduit function, which means that she must be identifiable with the agency of the white male viewer.

This complication is borne out by the structure of the gaze in the work. The servant's look does indeed initiate the movement in the painting: it creates a vector that begins with the servant's sidelong glance at the naked woman, who turns it outward, towards the viewer, creating another formal triangle. In a nude such as the *Venus Anadyomène*, this triangle would begin with the viewer, go through the stand-in figure(s), and culminate in the nude, the object of desire. Here, however, the viewer is the third and final point in this vector, the object gazed at (not only by the nude but, by proxy, by the servant also) rather than the gazer. The disconcerting nature of Olympia's direct stare, then, is that it constructs the egoistic gaze as originating with a woman and culminating in a man, when the pleasure of the male viewer depends on the fact that 'the male figure cannot bear the burden of sexual objectification'.[16]

Even if the nudity of the white woman in the painting were enough to construct her as the object of desire in spite of her position *vis-à-vis* the male gaze, however, the presence of the black woman still subverts the visual pleasure of the male viewer unbearably. Her position defines his, as Ann Kaplan claims: 'the look of the male spectator . . . imitates (or is necessarily in the same position as)' that of the 'stand-in' within the image.[17] The unignorable specificity of the black woman in terms of race and gender in the painting make it impossible for the male viewer to pleasurably identify her as 'like' him. Yet her formal position insists upon this identification, endowing her with the agency of the (male) sexual subject because structurally she is identical with him.

To summarize these two arguments, then: if the black woman is the desiring subject (because of her analogous position to the white male sexual agent) and the object of her desire the white woman (because of the hegemony of the convention of the nude), a heretofore unrecognized motive for contemporary disgust with the painting emerges. Gilman points out that 'the concupiscence of the black is . . . associated with the sexuality of the lesbian'[18] in nineteenth-century iconography. The prostitute is also consistently associated with what we would today call the lesbian, with whom she shares 'physical signs that set [her] apart from the normal'.[19] In making a different argument, Gilman claims that the two figures in the painting are juxtaposed in such a way as to 'imply a similarity between the sexuality of the two'.[20] I would suggest that this similarity might include the representation of lesbianism.[21] Formally, too, the painting suggests that the desire in the painting exists between the two women. The composition of the work enacts a distracting splitting of the classic pyramid form. As we see in the *Venus Anadyomène* and even in Manet's own *Déjeuner*, the pyramid form allows the eye to unite all the elements of the painting in a single glance. The image is thus appropriable, commodified, an object of easy consumption. *Olympia*, on the other hand, presents the viewer with two equally viable pyramid forms: that created by Olympia's head and torso and the pillow, and that of the black servant's head and body, the base of which consists of Olympia's calves and the cat's body. Neither clearly takes precedence, leaving the viewer without an easy way visually to appropriate the image. Between these two pyramids is a third, to be sure, an upside-down pyramid: the empty space the perimeter of which runs from the servant's head to Olympia's, down her arm to her hand and back up her thigh and the servant's body. But this is not a good compositional form, whole and easily visualized: it is an inverted parody, a vacuum. Its disturbing emptiness emphasizes its perimeter and apexes, especially that over-marked hand of Olympia's that aroused such disgust when it was first seen. That hand, as Clark points out, is a too-visible sign of Olympia's feminine sexuality. Its positivity indicates that there are active, working genitals behind it, not the smooth blank between the legs of the *Venus Anadyomène*. But there is another, equally emphatic hand in the painting to which Olympia's refers: it is that of the black woman, sharply outlined against the white paper surrounding the bouquet.[22] The juxtaposition of the white hand as a marker of feminine sexuality with the equally strong black hand metonymically endows the latter with sexual significance. The position of the two hands on the edge of the triangle, forced upon our attention by the fact that we literally cannot look at its empty interior, suggests a sexual connection between the two women much as do their gazes, also fixed at key points in the central triangle. This lesbian desire between the two women is a further mechanism for excluding and thus denying agency to the desire of the bourgeois white male: in fact, the radical incoherence of the intersection of female desire in the painting may well represent the limits of my own argument as well. I do not mean this to indicate a weakness in my reading of lesbian desire in *Olympia*: on the contrary, incoherence is the inevitable marker of the oppositional limits of a given discourse, and hence definitive of that discourse and its object.

For this incoherence certainly does mark a limit. Given Mulvey's and Kaplan's arguments, I cannot simply assert that the black servant is an agent of desire in this painting. Such a statement would be extremely problematic in the context of a form (the nude) developed to accommodate the desire of the bourgeois white male. Clark points out that *Olympia* was, after all, painted as a nude and ultimately consumed as one.[23] It is unlikely that 1865 viewers, as a result of the formal undermining described above, would conclude that black women are sexual agents just as are white men. Rather, this displacement of agency on to the doubly marginalized, almost invisible figure in the painting works to undercut the notion of agency itself. In other words, since a black woman cannot be conceived as an agent in the context of the nude, when agency is shifted to such a figure it ceases to work as agency. Rather than initiating meaning in the painting, as the white male gaze would have, the black woman's oblique glance swallows it up in a paradigmatic expression of the insatiability for which she was conventionally reviled.

In the context of the nude, then, the only agency possible is that of the bourgeois white male. The nude cannot construct another subject: if a painting is to displace coherent bourgeois subjectivity, it must do so by making it uncomfortable or impossible in a specific viewing moment. If the nude were to try to construct another subjectivity, such an alternative would inevitably be defused by the inability of the 1865 viewer to *see* a courtesan or a black maidservant as an agent. This is the dilemma of the avant-garde: it is not enough simply to create a new concept of subjectivity, for unless the historical moment exists in which that concept can be seen and recognized, it will always be co-opted by existing conditions. It will, however, displace those conditions somewhat. Manet's painting, then, despite the fact that through its formal structures it robs the bourgeois male of his subjectivity and guarantees the black woman hers, was unable to do so historically. What it did, perhaps, was aid in the construction of the historical moment in which the bourgeois white male subject *would* be successfully deconstructed.

But what are the limits of art as political agent? Georg Lukács, one of the early combatants in this modernist fray, reminds us that any new form 'is not only a result but also and simultaneously a cause' in history.[24] When a potentially disruptive work of art is viewed, 'an interaction always takes place'[25] not only between the work and the viewer but also between the viewer and the social whole. Thus, we can understand the historically determined constraints on the political potential of Manet's art. John Richardson refers to the well-known apocrypha that despite his revolutionary formal gestures, Manet was the ultimate *bourgeois* whose iconoclastic art was compromised by 'a desire for conventional success'[26] and a craving for the medal of the Legion of Honour. He wanted to exhibit in the Salon proper, not the *Salon des Refusés* where his Impressionist contemporaries gloried in their avant-garde isolation.[27] Manet's 'politics' were formal only: he was funda-mentally uninterested in the potentially explosive effect of his art. Thus, he takes the limitations of his public (in terms of gender, sexuality, class, and race) for granted: he does not pose 'who consumes' as a problem. And even if he had been so interested, in the Salon context situated and in large part defined by the institutions of academic painting and of bourgeois cultural acquisition, all his painting can do is to articulate the limits of bourgeois desire. It cannot constitute an alternative formation, and it cannot truly explode that desire, which is instantiated and supported by the viewer's very presence in the Salon. What it can do, however, is suggest that there *is* something beyond the desire of the bourgeois white male, that this desire is not as seamless and universal as capitalist patriarchy needs it to appear. Such a suggestion, in such a context, is necessarily almost incomprehensible; hence, it is marked by incoherence. The possibility of desire on the part of the racial or sexual Other, as my analysis above suggests, is contradictory and self-subverting. This is how we know that it is at the edge of the possible for the bourgeois white male viewer.

Cornell University

NOTES

This paper was written for a seminar on Marxism and Modernism at Cornell University, Spring 1987. My theoretical understanding of modernism and of representation is deeply indebted to the collective work of this class. I would also like to acknowledge Paisley Currah, Biddy Martin, Satya Mohanty, Derek Spitz, Sasha Torres, Ann Wilson, and Álok Yadav, all of whom read and generously commented upon drafts of this paper.

1 Eunice Lipton, for example, contends that Manet's depictions of women present strong, assertive figures in active roles, in contrast to traditional art historical images of weak and passive women. (E. Lipton, 'Manet: a radicalized female imagery', *Artforum* (March 1977), pp. 48–53.)
2 T. J. Clark, *The Painting of Modern Life: Paris in the Art of Manet and his Followers* (Princeton: Princeton University Press, 1984), 108.

3 ibid., 118.

4 Alain Corbin notes how the ideology surrounding prostitution in nineteenth-century France 'integrates the prostitute with that chain of resigned female bodies, originating in the lower classes and bound to the instinctive physical needs of the upper-class males' (p. 212). He traces the development of the bourgeois male from his place at the nurse's breast, through the intimate ministrations of the nursery maid and the sexual services of the 'Martha/Mary Magdalen' figure of the housemaid, to his servicing by the old servant maid who waits to lay out his dead body. (Alain Corbin, 'Commercial sexuality in nineteenth-century France: a system of images and regulations', *Representations*, 14 (1986), pp. 209–19.)

5 Clark, op. cit., 135.

6 ibid., 135.

7 ibid., 136.

8 ibid., 137.

9 Clark's analytic categories (or category – he seems able to account for subjectivity, as I am arguing, *only* in terms of class) can also be successfully challenged by feminist ideology critique. Because of its close relation to twentieth-century Marxism, this branch of feminist analysis might seem closer to Clark's own project and therefore a more legitimate position from which to critique it. Although the recent work of Cora Kaplan (*Sea Changes*, 1986) and Seyla Benhabib and Drucilla Cornell (*Feminism as Critique*, 1987) offer crucial formulations of current feminist categories of subjectivity (such as gender, sexuality, race, and class) in general, I feel that such work still leaves too large a gap between theoretical, categorical considerations and material analysis of a visual or verbal text. Teresa de Lauretis, in *Technologies of Gender* (1987), has managed to develop a theoretical paradigm that accounts for all of these categories of subjectivity *and* for the texts in which they are produced – but her work, too, exploits the insights of Lacanian psychoanalysis. (S. Benhabib and D. Cornell, *Feminism as Critique* (Minneapolis: University of Minnesota Press, 1987); C. Kaplan, *Sea Changes: Essays on Culture and Feminism* (London: Verso, 1986); T. de Lauretis, *Technologies of Gender: Essays on Theory, Film and Fiction* (Bloomington: Indiana University Press, 1987).)

10 M. Fried, 'Manet's sources: aspects of his art, 1859–1865', *Artforum* (March 1969), p. 63.

11 A. Kaplan, 'Is the gaze male?' in A. Snitow *et al.*, *Powers of Desire: The Politics of Sexuality* (New York: Monthly Review Press, 1983), p. 311.

12 Fried, op. cit., p. 61.

13 L. Mulvey, 'Visual pleasure and narrative cinema', in B. Wallis (ed.), *Art After Modernism: Rethinking Representation* (New York: New Museum of Contemporary Art, 1984), p. 368.

14 S. Gilman, *Difference and Pathology: Stereotypes of Sexuality, Race and Madness* (Ithaca, NY: Cornell University Press, 1985), p. 79.

15 ibid.

16 Mulvey, op. cit., p. 367.

17 A. Kaplan, op. cit., p. 311.

18 Gilman, op. cit., p. 89.

19 ibid., p. 98.

20 ibid., p. 81.

21 The term 'lesbian' refers here only to my reading; the term did not come into

use until the end of the nineteenth century and so cannot refer to the content of the painting as contemporaries would have seen it. The homoerotic content, however, *was* available to Salon viewers even if the term we would now use for it was not.

22 Clark follows the contemporary critics he cites in considering the black hand against the white background a shadowy 'clipped and abstract silhouette' (p. 138), revealing the inability of both the 1865 viewer and Clark's analysis to recognize the manifest sexual signification (based on Clark's own argument) of the sharply visible black hand.

23 Clark, op. cit., p. 131.

24 G. Lukács, *Writer and Critic and Other Essays* (London: Merlin Press, 1970), p. 127.

25 ibid.

26 J. Richardson, *Manet* (London: Phaidon, 1967), p. 6.

27 ibid.

SCOTT WILSON

Racked on the tyrant's bed: the politics of pleasure and pain and the Elizabethan sonnet sequences

Magna est veritas, et praevalet.

I

In the 1580s and 1590s the officially sanctioned use of torture reached a peak in English history. During the same two decades the fashion for sonnet sequences, the most substantial contribution to the 'golden' era of lyric poetry, was also at its height.

This is an essay about intimate space, about constriction, coercion and the production of desire. I want to look at how the public realm acts on the 'soul' or conscience by writing it in a discourse of the body: its sexual pleasures and its pain.

If the state execution, with its display of public mutilation as a demonstration of sovereign power, can in its theatricality be compared to Elizabethan drama, then in some respects, I believe, state torture can be compared to the making of sonnets. Torture was a secret and secluded practice. Comparatively it did not happen all that often: even at its peak in the 1580s and 1590s its annual occurrence is minuscule compared to the number of around 800 executions a year. The production and reading of sonnets was also a marginal activity practiced by a relatively small elite. Like the confessions of a torture victim the reading of a sonnet was attended to by a small coterie audience of interested parties.

Although there is a significant number of names on torture warrants issued at this time, the names of the famous Elizabethan sonneteers do not feature among them.[1] Sidney, Daniel, Drayton, and Shakespeare were not, it seems, tortured poets. But the language of torture, of being tortured, sometimes in quite graphic detail, appears frequently in the sonnets. In elaborate conceits, hyperbole and metaphor a knowledge of torture is inscribed in the English rewriting of the Petrarchan sonnet convention. The metaphorical torment of the Petrarchan lover is literalized by Elizabethan sonnet makers in a way that has been described as 'grotesque'.[2] This tendency, seemingly peculiar to the English sequences, is evident as early as Wyatt's translations of Petrarch. The metaphysical pain of Laura's afflicted lover is translated as physical torment in concrete images of despair.[3] In two of Wyatt's love sonnets that appear in Tottel's *Songes and Sonettes*, which are not translations of Petrarch, Wyatt goes further and writes of 'chained prisoners' and 'Torments that prick more sharper than stele'.[4]

The Elizabethan sonnet sequences privilege the self. They manifest a desire to utter the truth of the self again and again in diverse combinations. In the sonnets I shall be examining this truth is produced by torture. The language of treason, the rack, torture, and confession is written in a discourse of truth, structured along the poles of love, desire, and the flesh. To complement this analysis – and to form an elaborate conceit of my own – I shall be making links between the sonnets themselves and other contemporary utterances that speak the language of torture. In ostensibly unrelated texts I will attempt to locate subject positions and changes in the forces that construct subjectivity. At the intersections of religious, political and legal discourses, beneath the fracturing light of truth and knowledge, I shall try to map the subterranean movements of power.

Of all the official torture warrants, over 60 per cent concern state crime: the activities of subversives, Catholic priests, and plotters. Power, in the unrelated texts I shall be concerned with, is defined in analogous terms. While the amorous subject of the sonnet is racked on a paradox as cruel chastity tears at fleshly desire, textualized versions of state torture write agony in a similar way: sedition is written as seduction; punishment and torture are applied for 'lewdness' in the face of a gracious Queen. In these texts sexual, political, and religious differences are collapsed into oppositional relations of fear. The result is a remarkably paradoxical discourse that in its literary utterances has virginal women torturing the souls of Protestant civil servants, whilst in state prisons similarly disposed males tortured the bodies of Catholics in the name of a virgin.

II

In 1619, nearly twenty years after the fashion for sonnet sequences had died down, Ben Jonson reflected upon his life and art. In conversations recorded by William Drummond, Jonson interspersed revealing information about his own early imprisonment and Catholic conversion with opinions on the work and reputation of his fellow poets. In particular Drummond records that Jonson 'cursed Petrarch for redacting verses to sonnets which, he said, were like that Tirrant's bed, wher some who were too short were racked, others too long cut short'.[5] This witty image is suggestive of the sonnet's formal constrictions. But a *tyrant*'s bed might also be construed as an arena of political normalization manipulating sexual pleasures and pain. Unfortunately, like many of Jonson's remarks, this one, it seems, is not original. Sir Sidney Lee, the eminent Victorian critic whose life's work was apparently dedicated to demonstrating the extent of Elizabethan poets' borrowing from their much cleverer French and Italian contemporaries, revealed to *The Atheneum* in 1904 that Jonson 'was merely repeating in his own language the comment of Stephano Guazzo'.[6] In the 7th Dialogue of Guazzo's *Dialoghi Piacenoli* one of the interlocutors comments on the difficulty inherent in the sonnet form:

> It seems to me that signor Claudio Tolomei had reason for saying that the sonnet was like the bed of Procrustes. Procrustes was so eccentric and brutal that all travellers who came to his inn were made to lie down in a certain bed, and from those whose length of body went beyond the bed he cut off the legs to suit the bed's dimensions, but as for those who were too short, he stretched their necks and legs with cords so that they might precisely fit the bed's size. And since it is almost impossible to find a subject which exactly fits the frame of the sonnet, it is imperative either to add idle words, or to break off the conceits in such a manner that the composition becomes either idle or obscure.[7]

It has been argued that the sonnet's formal difficulties are so severe that even the greatest of Shakespeare's 'are flawed by a discrepancy between form and idea'.[8] However, it is not only the formal difficulties of the sonnet that make the image of the torturing bed an appropriate one. In a sonnet sequence the manifold ambivalences of Petrarchan love are delicately structured in intricate patterns. Pleasure and pain are eroticized in countless examples of paradox and oxymoron. The subject, feeling love as hate, fire as ice, is cursed in bliss; day is experienced as night and presence as absence. The mistress, of whom and to whom most of the sonnets are addressed, is cited as an absent presence, an image inscribed in the heart of the lover, internalized as a defining other, an object around which subjectivity is formed. The lover's subjection is agonizingly pleasurable, not only to the self, but also, hopefully, to the cruel mistress herself. From the beginning of Sidney's sequence Astrophil's intention is that his torment be written for the pleasure of his beloved. In the first sonnet he expresses the hope that Stella may read and enjoy the agony she produces. He writes:

> That she (dear she) might take some pleasure of my paine,
> Pleasure might cause her read, reading might make her know,
> Knowledge might pitie winne, and pittie grace obtain[9]

With the confession of his sufferings, Astrophil projects on to his mistress the power over his struggles of conscience. She can bestow or withdraw 'grace': an ambivalent term designating either sexual or spiritual bliss. Yet Stella's supposed power is based on Astrophil's knowledge of his own self. This is a subjectivity he forms in language, stretched and compressed on the self-made rack of the sonnet's tight block of text. Stella has no power to form utterances; it is not her discourse.

In this sense the sonnet, as a mode of discourse, is different from the genealogically related mode of the Catholic confessional. In the wake of

Foucault there has been much critical interest in making the analogy between the Petrarchan love lyric and the confessional.[10] In the confessional the subject confesses sins before the Virgin but speaks the discourse of the Church. The intimacies uttered in the tight space of the confessional box (which was introduced in the sixteenth century)[11] are controlled and sanctioned by the silent and knowing priest. The Christian pastoral, according to Foucault, produces 'specific effects on desire, effects of mastery and detachment, but also an effect of blissful suffering from feeling in one's body the pangs of temptation and the love that resists it'.[12] As can be seen in Foucault's use of a Petrarchan oxymoron ('blissful suffering') the same effects occur in the secular discourse. This similarity would be exploited in the Tower when the state interrogators sought to press on English Catholics an allegiance to another virgin.

The difference for the confessing subjects of the sonnet sequence is that their 'self-knowledge' is for the most part represented as an internal, intimate possession. The amorous subject of a sonnet sequence is detached from an external arbiter. The audience or reader of the sonnet would be, I suppose, the analogous figure to the priest, but does not have the same authoritative role. The 'I' of the sonnet utterance is a configuration of both the Protestant 'I' and the Petrarchan 'I', both self-obsessed and self-determining: they make their own bed and they writhe about on it alone. This is Astrophil on his:

> Ah bed, the field where joye's peace some do see,
> . . . With sweet soft shades thou oft invitest me
> To steale some rest, but wretch I am constrained,
> (Spur'd with love's spur, though gald and shortly raind
> With care's hard hand) to turne and tosse in thee,
> While the blacke horrors of the silent night
> Paint woes blacke face so lively to my sight,
> . . . But when Aurora leades out Phœbus' daunce,
> Mine eyes then only winke, for spite perchance
> That wormes should have their Sun, and I want mine.[13]
> (Sidney, Sonnet 98, lines 1, 5–10, 12–14)

If there is an external arbiter to the speaker of the sonnet sequence, it is the bed of language itself and the conceptual schemes that regulate it. The subject is variously racked across paradoxes, binary oppositions that 'care' with a 'hard hand', 'constrain' and 'spur' the subject in a torment of contradictions. In Elizabethan sonnets the ordering principle that holds these contradictions together is light – the sun, signifier of life, power, truth, and sovereignty. 'Light', Derrida has noted, 'has perhaps no opposite; if it does, it is certainly not night.'[14] The shadow and darkness that is the context for Astrophil's waking, nocturnal struggle is produced by the light of the sun, which, like Stella herself, reveals and conceals itself in a circle of day and night, presence and absence. The metaphor Astrophil makes between Stella and the sun works both ways: they refer to each other. Stella's light, which Astrophil aims to possess, is of the same stuff as the sovereign light of the sun, the light of power and truth that orders even the worms. Stella, however, is an individualized light; her image is inscribed in Astrophil's heart and represents a personal truth. This personal truth operates with the same logic as sovereign truth: it desires to possess and control; ultimately it seeks to eclipse with its power the light and alterity of the other. 'If the other could be possessed, seized and known, it would not be the other. To possess, to grasp, to know are all synonyms of power.'[15]

Similar 'heliopolitics', it appears, operated as part of the black horrors of the torture chamber beneath the Tower and at Bridewell. According to an addendum to an anonymous state propaganda pamphlet, attributed to William Cecil, *The Execution of Justice in England*, the scene of Elizabethan torture was, it seems, lit by the radiant image of a virgin woman in order to inspire Catholic confessors to detach themselves from their faith and betray their fellows. The addendum, *A Declaration of the favourable dealing of Her Majesty's Commissioners appointed for the examination of certain traitors and of tortures unjustly reported to be done upon them for matters of religion*, is considered to have been written by Thomas Norton, co-author of *Gorboduc* and known notoriously by Catholics as 'Rackmaster General'.[16] In the text there is a description of the delicacies of the torture procedure which produces a macabre parallel to the Petrarchan scene of agony:

> the proceeding to torture was always so slowly [begun], so unwillingly and with so many preparations of persuasions to spare themselves . . . even in the necessary use of such proceeding [it] is nevertheless to be acknowledged the sweet temperature of Her Majesty's mild and gracious clemency and their slanderous lewdness.[17]

It was a comfort, no doubt, as your limbs were extended and the joints began to crack, to be reminded of Her Majesty's 'sweet temperature' and her 'gracious clemency'. The point, needless to say, of the invocation here of Elizabeth in her familiar guise of Virgin Queen is to erase the political nature of the scene and rewrite resistance in moral terms as 'slanderous lewdness'. It is a strategy that works on a moral-religious discourse of sin, grace, and clemency familiar to the Catholic confessors, but legitimating and empowering the state. The ultimate aim is to eclipse the internal light of the Catholic other with the greater light of sovereign beauty and truth. That the means to the Catholic conscience is through the torment of the body is also, of course, part of the discourse.

Those 'lewd' Catholics who evaded the clutches of the state happily did not, according to William Cecil, escape this bodily torment. Charles Neville, the leader of the 1569 Rising in the North, is said by Cecil to be 'a person utterly wasted by looseness of life . . . his body is now eaten with ulcers of lewd causes'.[18] There is a paradox in this state writing of Catholic recusants. They are both enlisted as subjects of the same erotico-political discourse and projected as an alien other, frightening, foreign, and debauched. This contradiction runs throughout *The Execution of Justice*: Catholics are both other and the same.

The pamphlet was of great importance to the state. Robert Kingdon in his introduction to the text stresses that 'this book, although slight in size and crabbed in style . . . was widely circulated and possessed an official character.'[19] It was translated into Latin, French, German, Dutch, Italian, and possibly Spanish. English diplomats at the time were furnished with copies to present to the governments to which they were assigned. The reason for such a wide distribution, especially on the continent, seems to have been the English government's sensitivity towards its neighbours.[20] France and Spain were both militantly Catholic and very powerful. The fear of foreign invasion was justifiably high in the English court in the 1580s; the combined power of France and Spain, sufficiently determined, would certainly have been overwhelming. Part of the project of Cecil's pamphlet was, then, to mitigate these fears by attempting to persuade the Kings of France and Spain, and the Holy Roman Emperor himself, that the English government tortured Catholics only on the grounds of sedition or treason and not for matters of conscience.

The Execution of Justice is a political text that seeks to justify itself, and the activities of the government it supports, in the terms of both legal and moral justice, while employing lies and slanderous rhetoric. Catholics certainly *were* tortured for their religious beliefs, and there is no evidence that the majority of their leaders were sexually depraved. The contradictions that rack Cecil's crabbed and tortured prose reveal the workings of a power that the subject of the utterance seems not to be aware of, since he is also affected by it. Behind Cecil's elision of the legal and moral discourses is a struggle for self-preservation and self-mastery analogous to that of the state. It is a conflict over what forms a conscience, what modes of truth, knowledge, and belief will get to power. Cecil's text elides the significations of truth and power. It is clear enough in his postscript which appropriates a biblical maxim for Elizabeth: '*Magna veritas, et praevalet.*' (Truth is great and she overcometh.) Cecil's text, and Norton's, present sovereign truth overcoming inexorably, though with reluctance, through torture.

III

Truth, beauty, light, and power are signs beneath which the Queen most wanted to be written. The metaphysical violence of such concepts, the pain and desire they effect and cause, was suffered — metaphorically at least — by all of Elizabeth's subjects, even those in high office and in the intimate circles of the court itself. The following quotation is a piece of political correspondence addressed to the Queen in 1573 by Sir Christopher Hatton, a future Privy Councillor, who seems, in this instance, to have been irresponsibly neglectful of Her Majesty's good graces:

Madame, I find the greatest lack that ever poor wretch sustained. No death, no hell, no fear of death shall ever win of me my consent so far to wrong myself again as to be absent from you one day . . . to serve you is a heaven, but to lack you is more than hell's torment. . . . Passion overcometh me. I can write no more. Love me; for I love you.[21]

It is wit, of course, and from a modern perspective grovelling flattery, but for the Catholics in the Tower the utterance contains an uncomfortable truth. Hatton declares that to wrong the Queen is to suffer the torment of the 'greatest lack'. The subject's self-presence is only possible when fully subjected to the full authority and power of the monarch. Not to be bathed in her sovereign light is to suffer the ultimate torment of spiritual non-being. It is worse than physical torture, worse than death, worse even than hell itself. The power of the Virgin Queen is truly awful, god-like, and Hatton is a mere wretch beside it. Yet Hatton's project is not just to flatter Elizabeth: he wants to promote and aggrandize himself. He needs to appear worthier in all respects than his political rivals. In this letter he is attempting to exploit the erotico-political power game that the Queen seemed to enjoy playing with her courtiers. He acts out his role and attempts to manoeuvre the Queen to a point in the discourse that will allow him certain masculine rights. As passion begins to overcome him and his utterance falters with emotion, he squares up to the monarch man-to-woman: 'Love me,' he demands, 'for I love you.' In the imperative mode of the last sentence the wretch becomes a lion.

The tyrannical power over life and death which Hatton invests in the Queen is also fully invested in the heroines of the sonnet sequences, and for the same reason, for the display and aggrandizement of the male self. In the sonnets, though, this tyrannical power is frequently written, no doubt for greater effect, in a more ambiguous way than would be prudent for a professional politician like Hatton. In Drayton's sonnet 20 of his *Idea* sequence the torturing beauty is fully demonized:

An evill spirit, your beauty haunts Me still,
Wherewith (alas) I have been long possest,
Which ceaseth not to tempt Me to each Ill
Nor gives Me once but one poor minutes rest:
In Me it speakes whether I sleepe or Wake,
And when by means to drive it out I try,
With greater Torments then it Me doth take,
And tortures Me in most extremity:
Before my Face it layes down my Despaires,
And hastes Me on to a sudden death,
Now tempting Me to drown my Selfe in teares,
And then in sighing, to give up my breath:
Thus am I still provoked to every Evill
By this good wicked Spirit, sweet Angell Devill.[22]

The male subject here is up against no less a power than the Prince of Darkness himself. In this elaborate conceit Drayton plays on the traditional temptations to suicide with which the Devil attacks the person in despair. But it is not the Devil here, it is the speaker himself, faced with himself and his relationship with his own idealized piece of refracted beauty. This meditation on despair foregrounds the astonishing discursive paradox that projects beauty and transcendent truth not only on that which is other and unknown, but also onto that which is negative, dark, irrational and, here, evil. The speaker imagines himself possessed by a peculiar 'Angell Devill', a splinter of dark light that works relentlessly to undermine his selfhood. It gives him not 'one poor minutes rest', it speaks through him, it seems part of him. The schizophrenic struggle for self-government only produces more torture: 'Before my Face it layes down my Despaires'. It holds a mirror to the self-denying circularity of the speaker's subjectivity. Within this circle the only act of resistance is one which is simultaneously self-assertive and self-denying. It is to rebel against the rule of law and usurp 'the power of life and death which the sovereign alone, whether the one here or the Lord above, has the right to exercise'.[23] In the circle of individualism that the sonnet produces the only subversive act is suicide.

When I have employed this metaphor of light, and foregrounded the friendship between light and power, I have not meant to suggest that power radiates from a singular, central point, for example from the sovereign or the state institutions. Light, like power, is ubiquitous but not centralized; it reflects and refracts in innumerable areas casting shade and shadow. Though the sun may be considered the source of all light and life,

> the most natural, most universal, most real, most luminous thing, the apparently most exterior referent, [it] does not completely escape the general law of metaphorical value as soon as it intervenes (as it always does) in the process of axiological and semantic value: 'The value of just any term is accordingly determined by its environment; it is impossible to fix the value of the signifier "sun" without considering its surroundings.'[24]

The sixteenth century did not, in any case, consider the sun to be the only source of light: the crystal spheres, stars, even the eyes of Petrarchan heroines were written as the source of their own radiating light.

Power, like light, was never centralized. The monarchy attempted to transcend the multiplicity of powers by identifying its will with the law, by writing itself in a juridico-political dimension and by establishing a cultural hegemony. The state amassed clusters of signs and notions that could cohere around and legitimate the monarchy: truth, light, beauty, the neo-Platonic ideal of reason, were all inscribed in the formations of Elizabeth as Virgin Queen and, famously in the 'Rainbow' portrait, as the sun itself.[25] Monarchs, however, can neither guarantee nor fix the significations of their cultural products. They cannot invent discourse, they cannot authorize or control language. Their power, like all power, is non-subjective; it is intentional to the extent that no power is exercised without a series of aims and objections, but it does not result from the choice or decision of an individual subject, not even when the subject is also the monarch.[26]

According to Foucault power is not articulated by law, the monarch's basic form of acceptability: 'The history of the monarchy went hand in hand with the covering up of the facts and procedures of power by juridico-political discourse.'[27] Power moves in the shadows of sovereign light, occasionally working in the name of the monarchy with the effect of undermining it. Similarly the cultural products that appertain to the monarchy do not unequivocally maintain it. The significations of the Petrarchan convention that were Elizabeth's main mode of manifestation, allow for desire, cruelty, and evil. These darker areas, as representations, leave space for suggestions concerning the very sensitive area of sovereign lawlessness. The unconstitutional activity of torture which was practised by state officers under the cover of the Royal Prerogative, was written as part of beauty's power.

The last twenty-seven sonnets of Shakespeare's sequence fully exploit the dark side of the Petrarchan convention. In these sonnets 'beauty herself is black' (132: 13); she is mendacious, immoral, and foul. The dark beauty imprisons and tortures the hearts of her subjects after they have been caught in the snares of desire and sex. Sonnet 133 of the sequence adopts the torturing conceit to this effect:

> Beshrew that heart that makes my heart to groan
> For that deep wound it gives my friend and me.
> Is't not enough to torture me alone,
> But slave to slavery my sweet'st friend must be?
> Me from myself thy cruel eye hath taken,
> And my next self thou harder hast engrossed.
> Of him, myself, and thee, I am forsaken –
> A torment thrice threefold to be crossed.
> Prison my heart in thy steel bosom's ward,
> But then my friend's heart let my poor heart bail;
> Whoe'er keeps me, let my heart be his guard,
> Thou canst not then use rigour in my jail.
> And yet thou wilt, for I being pent in thee
> Perforce am thine, and all that is in me.[28]

The tangle of conflicting powers that are projected, suffered and exerted in this grim sexual ménage are controlled by the laws of the erotico-political discourse. It is beauty, the law-giver, who is projected as the cause, through her own immorality, of the series of betrayals that has led to the sufferings of the speaker and his friend. This dark mistress is both the architect of crime and its jailer; she has the keys to the state prison and the means to adopt 'rigour' in the pursuit of allegiance and possession. The legal and moral ambiguity of this 'Petrarchan' heroine, one who 'sweares she is made of truth' and yet lies consistently (138: 1–2), is a very dangerous notion to a Queen who wished to be written into the convention herself.

IV

English state torture was strictly speaking illegal and constitutes one of sovereign beauty's blacker shadows. The reason why torture was never an accepted judicial process, John Langbein suggests, was not that the English were possessed with 'any unusual degree of humanity or enlightenment'.[29] Rather, they were the beneficiaries of legal institutions, like the jury system, so crude that torture was unnecessary: 'to this day an English jury can convict a defendant on less evidence than was required as a mere precondition for interrogation under torture on the continent.'[30] Since judicial torture was not felt to be needed, it was never formally legalized. Consequently the state was very sensitive to accusations concerning its use on English subjects. Indeed the existence of torture was frequently officially denied, even by those who took part in it. Sir Thomas Smith in 1565 and Sir Edward Coke in 1620, both of whom were designated in commissions to examine subjects under torture, deny its use in England. William Cecil's *Execution of Justice*, which admits of a few extraordinary cases, was produced as a defensive response to the increasing volume of Catholic complaints. The eighty-one instances for which there are official warrants were applied by a special use of the Royal Prerogative whereby the individual agents of torture were granted the sovereign's immunity from prosecution.

The foreign, continental practice of judicial torture, though outside English law, was used in extraordinary circumstances as a supplement to it. English torture can be read as 'a dangerous supplement' in the Derridean sense.[31] The supplement is a dangerous means, a menacing aid to a situation of distress. If the equivocations of Cecil's text (and Norton's supplement to it) are anything to go by, then the use of torture seems to have been perceived as a transgressive action which was experienced with culpability. The law was meant to be the manifestation of the sovereign's will: the mode of the monarch's presence throughout the realm. When the law fails to protect that presence, when subversives cannot be stopped through legal means, then torture becomes necessary; it must be added to the law urgently. The supplement is dangerous, according to Derrida, precisely because it supplements: 'it adds only to replace. It intervenes or insinuates itself in-the-place of; if it fills, it is as if one fills a void.'[32] The individual power of the monarch is a void since power is always delegated into the hands of others, deferred through a chain of supplements:

> The supplement will always be the moving of the tongue or acting through the hands of others. In it everything is brought together: progress as the possibility of perversion, regression towards an evil that is not natural and that adheres to the power of substitution that permits us to absent ourselves and act by proxy, through representation, through the hands of others.[33]

Sir Francis Bacon, who was at least five times a participant – a mediating presence – in investigation under torture, wrote in a memorandum to King James that 'in the highest cases of treasons, torture is used for discovery and not for evidence'.[34] The kind of 'discovery' and the forms that it took were, it seems, quite varied. Since Catholics were not tortured for information concerning their guilt or for evidence that could lead to a conviction, there was some controversy over not only the general purpose of torture, but also the specific content of the confessions it was used to elicit. In a reply to Cecil's *Execution of Justice*, William Allen published, also anonymously, *A Defence of English Catholics* which is a point-by-point refutation of the government pamphlet, very well written with detailed evidence from Catholic confessors racked by the state. Allen produces testimony that suggests that the sort of knowledge that the interrogators sought to discover went far beyond the identification of fellow conspirators and future plots. The following is an account by Thomas Cottam S. J., who was tortured and executed in the spring of 1582:

> Indeed you are searchers of secrets, for you would needs know of me what penance I was enjoined by my ghostly father for my sins committed. And I acknowledge my frailty that to avoid the intolerable torment of the rack I confessed (God forgive me) what they demanded therein. But when they further urged me to utter also what my sins were for which that penance was enjoined me (a loathesome and unchristian question), I then answered that I would not disclose my offenses saving to God and my ghostly father alone. Whereupon they sore tormented me and still pressed me with the same demand. And I persisted that it was a most barbarous, inhumane question and that I would not answer though they tormented me to death.[35]

It seems a strange sort of knowledge that the interrogators are seeking here. Matters of treason have apparently been suspended: the whereabouts of plotters, wanted Jesuits, safe houses and so on are not in question. The commissioners are interested in the content of Cottam's most recent confessions, and the penance he has subsequently made. From Cottam's outraged and determined reaction it seems they were intruding on the black secrets of his conscience, seeking knowledge of the sins that soil a confessor's soul. What could have been the motive for such an apparently unusual direction of questioning? It may have been that they were looking for some evidence to back up the sort of slander that can be read in Cecil's pamphlet. From the twentieth-century perspective of torture the technique seems to be aimed at humiliation: a project to transfer the shame of the situation directly on to the prisoner.

The 'inhumane and barbarous' questions that appall Cottam are peculiarly modern in their intimacy and intrusiveness. The twentieth-century experience of torture bases its techniques on humanistic knowledges: on biology, anthropology, psychology and so on in order to capture and control the victim completely. 'In the twentieth-century,' according to Edward Peters, 'it is not primarily the victim's information but the victim that torture needs to win – or reduce to powerlessness.'[36]

Of course the modern experience can not be anachronistically compared with the sixteenth-century, but it is important to remember that English torture, though unconstitutional, was still employed in aid of a rational as opposed to a ritual mode of truth. It was never linked, as in Europe, with judicial games like court ordeals, tests, trials or judgements of God: 'The use of torture presupposed a legal system that wanted to base judgement on the truth in part by means of regulated coercion.'[37] There are two forms of truth, and power, concerned with the interrogation of Thomas Cottam. One is the truth of the self – the secrets – that the state wished to extract by regulated coercion, and the other is the truth that the state wished to instil and subject its prisoners to. The project, no doubt, was to make the two forms of truth synonymous. But is there a third form of knowledge and power concerned with Cottam's examination? Perhaps the figure of Francis Bacon takes on a certain significance here, as lawyer, empirical philosopher, and part-time torturer. In *The Advancement of Learning*, 'Discovery' (which Bacon suggested justified the use of torture) is opposed to 'Impression' and defined as a mode of human knowledge. Its first domain is that of physiognomy 'which discovereth the disposition of the mind by the lineaments of the body'.[38] Cottam's interrogators, as they racked and stretched his body, probed the darker realms of his mind.

Torture may have been textualized as a manifestation of sovereign power, but, as I have argued, torture was a secluded activity beyond and supplementary to the law. In this twilight area, in the shadows of sovereign immunity, it appears that state interrogators – and nascent empiricists like Bacon – exercised the regulated violence of their rationalism in the pursuit of knowledge.

This strange effect, where one epistemic moment appears in the shadows of another, is perfectly illustrated by sonnet 50 of Drayton's *Idea* sequence. It seems to refer to a very distinctive and unusual application of the French practice of *torture préalable*:

> As in some countries, farre remote from hence,
> The wretched creature, destined to die,
> Having the Judgement due to his Offence,
> By Surgeon's beg'd, their Arte on him to trie,
> Which on the Living work without remorse,
> First make incision on each mast'ring Veine,
> Then stanch the bleeding, then trans-pierce the Coarse,
> And with their balmes recure the wounds againe;
> Then poyson, and with Physike him restore:
> Not that they feare the hope-lesse Man to kill,
> But their Experience to increase the more:
> Ev'n so my Mistress works upon my Ill;
> By curing me, and killing me each How'r
> Only to show her Beauties Sov'raigne Pow'r.[39]

I have not been able to discover whether the peculiar and grisly practice described in this sonnet took place in England. The sonnet suggests that it occurs 'in some countries farre remote from hence', but as any reader of Elizabethan drama knows, what is represented as foreign frequently has some bearing closer to home. The situation that occupies the first twelve lines in such detail in this sonnet seems to be a confluence of at least two related practices. The first is the French use of *torture préalable* which involves torturing the prisoner after conviction, but before execution. According to Langbein,

> the criminal who had been duly convicted and was awaiting execution of a capital sentence had forfeited his life. Since the criminal was the state's to execute, the state might put him to some better use first. The doctrine developed prominently in France that the condemned criminal could be examined under torture.[40]

Whether this 'better use' involved medical practice I have yet to find out. It might seem, to the keen surgeon anxious to exercise Vesalius' ideal of 'living anatomy', a logical extension of the common sixteenth-century practice of supplying medical schools with the corpses of freshly executed prisoners; the recently established Royal College of Surgeons were allowed two corpses a year.

Interesting as it is, the contextual basis of the sonnet is not my primary concern here. What is also important is how the employment of such an elaborate conceit can so vividly locate an instance of apparent epistemic change. The sonnet presents a site of conflicting powers and knowledges: the cruelty of sovereign beauty co-exists uneasily with medical science increasing its 'Experience'.[41] The sonnet demonstrates a peculiar Elizabethan version of what Derrida calls 'the friendship between light and power, [and the] complicity between theoretical objectivity and technico-political possession'.[42] Scientific objectivity and subjective intentions emerge together in, and are formed by, the rules that structure social practices. These rules, the rule of law, truth, virtue, and goodness 'are empty in themselves, violent and unfinished; they are impersonal and can be bent to any purpose' in a strategy of domination.[43] In Drayton's sonnet the medical practitioners are represented as an example of the evil side of beauty's power. They are cited as a marginal, malevolent force. Within a hundred years or so it would be the science of 'enlightenment' represented by these practitioners that would lay claim to the authenticating rule of truth and progress.

Both torture and the sonnet sequence died out as English practices soon after the reign of Elizabeth ended. It is not my purpose to suggest that the end of the 'golden' era of the sonnet shows a decline in English lyric poetry, any more than the end of torture indicates some form of humanitarian progress. I have chosen to focus on these two marginal, supplementary practices because I believe they can be read as brief instances in the historical genealogy of the modern individual. Sonnets like Drayton's 50th in the *Idea* sequence write versions of the self produced through torture. Elizabethan state torture similarly constructed a form of subjectivity from those it subjected to its power. The confessions and the truth that the state produced under torture were prescribed precisely by what the state decided was a confession or what was the truth. Torture and confession – conventionally linked from the Greek as 'The Dark Twins' – have the same function: to transform a ruling discourse into subjectivity. It is in this way that 'truth overcometh'. The small group of lawyers and councillors that stood in the shadows while the torturer went about his business elicited the truth in a way analogous to the Father Confessors being racked. It was the listeners' discourse of truth that authenticated the speaking subject. Confessing the truth, whether a priest or a state interrogator, is inscribed, according to Foucault, 'at the heart of individualization by power'.[44] This power, it must be remembered, is unseen: delegated, substituted and deferred through the hands of others, power worked through the supplements of torture and writing.

State torture and Petrarchan sonnet sequences, as branches of the modern individual's family tree, produced nothing but bastard issue. It may be the case that it was the visible nature of their supplementarity that cut their brief, flourishing existences short, leaving the individualizing power to move on into new areas and new spaces. 'Blindness to the supplement' is, according to Derrida, a precondition to its existence.[45] Perhaps sonnet sequences and state torture became unable to sustain the illusion of presence. Each sonnet in a sequence supplements the other: one version of self-presence is replaced by another in a chain that simultaneously undermines the unity of the 'I' whilst promoting it. Torture was a dangerous means of supplementing sovereign presence-as-law that, because of its strict lawlessness, was also threatening, particularly when it became visible to both internal Catholic agitators and external foreign enemies alike. Importantly it is precisely this visibility (which perhaps proved to be the weakness of both practices) that can reveal the movement of power through the chain of supplements, and identify points of disruption and resistance.

In the myth of Procrustes no one escapes the strictures of the bed, not even Procrustes himself. When Thomas Norton, 'The Rackmaster General', wrote Walsingham his account of the torturing of Edmund Campion he was being confined, and made to speak, in prison.[46] Ben Jonson's analogy of the tyrant's bed identified an Elizabethan paradigm: it was on the rack of the sonnet and on the rack of the Tower that a certain anonymous, procrustean power sought to normalize subjects as loyal, obedient individuals.

University of Wales, Cardiff

NOTES

1 The eighty-one torture warrants surviving from the period 1540–1640 are cited in full by John H. Langbein, *Torture and the Law of Proof* (Chicago: University of Chicago Press, 1977), pp. 100–33.
2 Stephen Booth, *Shakespeare's Sonnets* (New Haven: Yale University Press, 1977), p. 460.
3 Compare, for example, the first quatrain of Petrarch's *Rime* 124 with Wyatt's translation, sonnet XXXI, in the Egerton Manuscript. Francesco Petrarch, *The Rime Sparse*, tr. Robert M. Durling (Cambridge, Mass.: Harvard University Press, 1976), pp. 238–9. Sir Thomas Wyatt, *Collected Poems*, ed. Kenneth Muir and Patricia Thomson (Liverpool: Liverpool University Press, 1969), p. 23.
4 Wyatt, *Collected Poems*, pp. 247–8.
5 *Ben Jonson, The Man and his Work*, ed. C. H. Herford and Percy Simpson (Oxford: Clarendon Press, 1925), p. 133.
6 Sir Sidney Lee, *The Atheneum* (9 July 1904), p. 49.
7 Stephano Guazzo cited Lee, ibid.
8 Philip Martin, *Shakespeare's Sonnets: Self, Love and Art* (Cambridge: Cambridge University Press, 1972), p. 105.
9 Sir Philip Sidney, *Selected Poems*, ed. Katherine Duncan-Jones (Oxford: Clarendon Press, 1979), p. 117.
10 See Stephen Greenblatt, *Renaissance Self-fashioning* (Chicago: University of Chicago Press, 1980), p. 117, and Gary Waller, *English Poetry of the Sixteenth Century* (New York: Longman, 1986), p. 102.
11 See John Bossy, 'The social history of confession in the age of the Reformation', *Transactions of the Royal Historical Society*, 5th series, 25, pp. 21–38.
12 Michel Foucault, *The History of Sexuality*, vol. 1, tr. Robert Hurley (Harmondsworth: Penguin Books, 1984), p. 23.
13 Sidney, *Selected Poems*, p. 181.
14 Jacques Derrida, 'Violence and metaphysics', in *Writing and Difference*, tr. Alan Bass (London: Routledge & Kegan Paul, 1981), p. 92.
15 Emmanuel Levinas cited Derrida, ibid.
16 See Conyers Read, 'William Cecil and Elizabethan public relations', in S. T. Bindoff, J. Hurstfield and C. H. Williams (eds), *Elizabethan Government and Society* (London: Athlone Press, 1961), p. 49.
17 See the Addendum to William Cecil, *The Execution of Justice in England*, ed. Robert M. Kingdon (Ithaca, NY: Cornell University Press, 1961), p. 49.
18 ibid., p. 4.
19 Langbein, op. cit., p. xvii.
20 See R. B. Wernham, 'Elizabethan war aims and strategy', in S. T. Bindoff *et al.* (eds), *Elizabethan Government and Society* (London: Athlone Press, 1961), pp. 340–68.
21 Sir Christopher Hatton, *Memoirs*, ed. Sir Harris Nicholas (London: Richard Bentley, 1847), pp. 26–7. See also Arthur F. Marotti, ' "Love is not love": Elizabethan sonnet sequences and the social order', *ELH*, 49 (1982), pp. 396–428, for a discussion of this and other instances of political correspondence.
22 Michael Drayton, *Elizabethan Sonnets*, ed. Maurice Evans (London: Dent, 1986), pp. 95–6.

23 Foucault, op. cit., p. 138.
24 Ferdinand de Saussure cited Jacques Derrida, 'The white mythology', in *Margins of Philosophy*, tr. Alan Bass (Brighton: Harvester, 1986), p. 219.
25 See Roy C. Strong, *The Portraits of Elizabeth I* (Oxford: Oxford University Press, 1963), pp. 84–6.
26 On non-subjective, intentional power see Foucault, op. cit., pp. 94–5.
27 ibid., p. 88.
28 William Shakespeare, *Sonnets*, ed. Stephen Booth (New Haven: Yale University Press, 1977), p. 115.
29 Langbein, op. cit., p. 77.
30 ibid., p. 78.
31 Jacques Derrida, ' "... That dangerous supplement ..." ', in *Of Grammatology*, tr. Gayatri Chakravorty Spivak (Baltimore: Johns Hopkins University Press, 1976), pp. 141–64.
32 ibid., p. 145.
33 ibid., p. 147.
34 Sir Francis Bacon, cited Langbein, op. cit., p. 90.
35 William Allen, *A Defence of English Catholics*, ed. Robert M. Kingdon (Ithaca, NY: Cornell University Press, 1965), p. 72.
36 Edward Peters, *Torture* (Oxford: Basil Blackwell, 1985), p. 165.
37 Langbein, op. cit., p. 77.
38 Sir Francis Bacon, *Of the Advancement of Learning*, Book II, in *Works*, vol. I (London, 1803), pp. 115–16.
39 Drayton, *Elizabethan Sonnets*, p. 108.
40 Langbein, op. cit., p. 16.
41 Francis Barker has noted a similar contradiction in Rembrandt's *The Anatomy Lesson*. See Francis Barker, *The Tremulous Private Body* (London: Methuen, 1984), p. 75.
42 Derrida, 'Violence and metaphysics', p. 91.
43 Michel Foucault, 'Nietzsche, genealogy, history', in *Michel Foucault: Language, Counter-Memory, Practice, Selected Essays and Interviews*, ed. D. F. Bouchard (Ithaca, NY: Cornell University Press, 1977), p. 151.
44 Foucault, *The History of Sexuality*, vol. 1, p. 59.
45 Derrida, ' "... That dangerous supplement ..." ', p. 149.
46 Norton had been imprisoned because of indiscreet manifestations of puritanism. His account is said to be the basis of his Addendum to Cecil's *The Execution of Justice*; see Conyers Read, 'William Cecil and Elizabethan public relations', p. 37.

RAYMOND WILLIAMS

The widely-lamented death last year of Raymond Williams has meant the loss of Britain's foremost contemporary socialist thinker. A Trust is being set up, with the status of a legal Charity, in order to fund a series of annual Memorial Lectures. These Lectures would discuss and develop the continuing relevance of his extraordinarily wide-ranging work to future cultural and political practice. They would be delivered in central London and the texts would be published.

We hope that many readers of *Textual Practice* will sympathise with this plan and contribute generously to its realisation. Cheques should be made out to 'Raymond Williams Memorial Trust' and sent to:

Graham Martin
Department of Literature
The Open University
Milton Keynes
MK7 6AA
GT. BRITAIN

Reviews

STEVEN RENDALL

● Reda Bensmaïa, *The Barthes Effect: The Essay as Reflective Text* (Minneapolis: University of Minnesota Press, 1987), 156 pp., $25.00

In a lecture delivered in 1977 on the occasion of his assumption of a chair of literary semiology in the Collège de France, Roland Barthes declared that 'Though it is true that I long wished to inscribe my work within the field of science – literary, lexicological, and sociological – I must admit that I have produced only essays, an ambiguous genre in which analysis vies with writing.'[1] Commenting on this declaration in her foreword to Reda Bensmaïa's study of Barthes and the essay, Michèle Richman asks how we are to interpret the self-deprecating 'only' – is it a deferential bow to science, an allusion to unfulfilled literary ambitions, or merely circumstantial modesty? None of these answers seems wholly satisfactory, as Richman indicates, if only because Barthes so often insisted on the 'responsibility of form'. Thus we 'must assume that his choice of a so-called ambiguous genre reflects a historically based decision as much as a personal predilection' (p. viii).

One might reply that Barthes's remark suggests that the essayistic character of his work became evident to him only *retrospectively*, when he recognized that he had failed to achieve his 'scientific' goals. The temptation to read this passage as reflecting a certain disillusionment and renunciation of earlier, inflated ambitions is strong – particularly for those who always thought Barthes something of a pretentious *littérateur*, and are only too ready to praise his humility in admitting that after all he had produced 'only essays'. Such an interpretation also meshes, of course, with the common view that after 1968 Barthes abandoned the acerbic social critique that had informed his early work, settled comfortably into the role of a former radical who had now seen the error of his youthful ways, and began to focus on bourgeois-humanist themes such as the individual, pleasure, and love. His acceptance of a chair in the Collège de France has been seen by both right- and left-wing critics as proof that in the end he returned to the bosom of the bourgeoisie.

But to adopt this perspective on Barthes's career is perhaps to blind oneself to the extent to which his practice of the essay in the last decade of his life can be considered a genuinely radical result of formal preoccupations that mark his writing from the outset. Reda Bensmaïa's book suggests that Barthes's recognition that he has produced 'only essays' amounts to a re-evaluation in which the essay appears as a privileged form that will allow him finally to realize his ambition 'to bring together in a single writing movement, in a single Text, modes of discourse that had hitherto been kept separate' (p. xxvi).

In the passage quoted above, Barthes situates the essay between the poles of *analysis* and *writing* (*écriture*); it is an 'ambiguous genre', a divided field on which opposing forces *vie*. Stressing the constitutive role of such divisions or differences in the Barthesian essay, Bensmaïa argues that the latter should be regarded neither as simply a mixture of genres nor as a dialectical resultant of the vectored forces composing it. Rather, Barthes invites us to recognize in the essay genre 'the matrix of all generic possibilities' (p. 92), the site of the *différance* (or 'structuration' or 'arche-writing') that is the precondition of any particular *kind* of discourse – including not only the traditional literary genres, but the discourses of science, politics, and literary theory as well.

Bensmaïa sees *S/Z* (1970) as a turning-point in Barthes's writing, and reads it as a proleptic theoretical commentary on the essays to come: *The Pleasure of the Text* (1973), *Roland Barthes by Roland Barthes* (1975), *A Lover's Discourse* (1977), and *Camera Lucida* (1980). He locates the Barthesian essay between the 'writerly text' and the 'readerly text', and argues that it executes the programme implicit in Barthes's description of an 'ideal text' in *S/Z*:

> Let us first posit the image of a triumphant plural, unimpoverished by any constraint of representation (of imitation). In this ideal text, the networks are many and interact, without any one of them being able to surpass the rest; this text is a galaxy of signifiers, not a structure of signifieds; it has no beginning; it is reversible; we gain access to it by several entrances, none of which can be authoritatively declared to be the main one; the codes it mobilizes extend *as far as the eye can reach* . . . (*S/Z*, pp. 5–6)

The name Bensmaïa proposes to give to this ideal is 'the reflective text'. As he points out, the word 'reflection' connotes not only 'thought' but also 'shimmering' or 'reverberation' (p. 105); and this suggests once again that the essay oscillates between *analysis* and *writing*.

Whereas 'analysis' or 'theory' (self-reflexion) implies the logical priority of one discourse or code with respect to another, the plural, decentred writing Barthes envisages constantly undoes such priorities: the differences it operates are reversible, it affords no single authoritative point of entry or exit, its codes can be neither arranged in a hierarchy nor contained within generic boundaries. In entering this field, analytical or theoretical concepts lose their authority and any fixed relation to other concepts within a given discourse (e.g. psychoanalysis, linguistics, semiotics); they become atopical, shimmering and reverberating among the plural networks of the 'reflective text'.

Now for all its apparent 'modernity', this way of undoing the hierarchy of discursive genres is characteristic of the essay from the beginning. We have only to remember how Montaigne's *Essays* incorporate the discourses of classical moral reflection, theology, law, medicine, cosmology, popular proverbial wisdom, etc., without granting any of them either inherent authority or priority over the others. His notorious practice of citation (usually without attribution and always without quotation marks, which were not yet an established typographical convention) lifts bits of these discourses out of their 'original' contexts, not in order to lend authority to his text, but to determine or rather *produce* his individuality – what we might call 'the Montaigne effect' – through the manner of their reinscription.

If the essay is born *practically and aesthetically* with Montaigne, Bensmaïa maintains that with Barthes it is reborn *theoretically* – because Barthes is the first to recognize its implications for a modern theory of the text. The essay returns, 'at another point on the spiral', as a *reflective text* that 'destroys utterly, *to the point of contradiction*, its own discursive category, its sociolinguistic reference (its "genre")' (p. 25, quoting Barthes, *The Pleasure of the Text*). 'Disconnected, mimed, mocked', fragments of all kinds of languages – including the 'theoretical' language of self-reflexive commentary – enter into the reflective text *on the same plane*.

While the field of the essay is thus *flat* (like the Robbe-Grilletian narrative without crucial scenes, in which everything is on the same level, etc.), it is not homogeneous. In fact – and this paradox is perhaps Bensmaïa's most important insight – the kind of unity peculiar to the essay as a genre depends upon the irreducible heterogeneity of its constituents.

Using Gilles Deleuze's concept of the 'dark precursor' or 'Differentiator', Bensmaïa is able to show that this mode of organization is already evident in Montaigne, where a 'sufficient word' generates two separate series. For instance, Montaigne's essay 'Of drunkenness' (which begins with the assertion that 'the world is nothing but variety and dissimilarity') seems to drift from a series of examples of the vice of drunkenness to divagations on Stoic heroism, the *furor poeticus*, and prophecy. Bensmaïa argues that

> Between the *signifying* series of 'vices' and the *signified* series of different types of 'intoxication' that Montaigne, seemingly improvisingly, parades before us, no equality, no semantic identity is established: of the two series paired by the dark precursor 'drunkenness', one always exceeds or stimulates the indeterminate character of the other. (p. 12)

The 'sufficient word' is thus not a clue to a single, hidden 'meaning' of the essay but rather the means of establishing the textual interference of two or more open-ended series. The essay's 'content' is contingent; what is constant and necessary is the mode of its structuration. Its logic is

> a logic of *complicatio*: through a paradoxical word heterogeneous series are put into communication and made to resonate without being subsumed. But there will always be a hiatus between the series, and only the 'sufficient' word will maintain a connection between them. . . . The aim is not to make the reader's task easier, but rather to teach how to decipher the signification of words that spring out of chaos and the 'perpetual movement' of all things. (p. 13)

In the Barthesian essay Montaigne's 'sufficient word' (which varies from one context to another) becomes a 'mana-word' operating everywhere to produce a fundamental difference or gap: the word 'body' (*corps*). It has this effect because, as Barthes – echoing Lacan, of course – reminds us in *The Pleasure of the Text*, we have more than one body. The erotic body of desire is irreducible to the physiological body of need, and this discontinuity is constitutive of the textual corpus:

> Barthes does not rely on the mana-word 'body' to designate a first or final signified; the essential function of the mana-word is to express a 'primary intensity' as pure difference that always puts (at least) two heterogeneous series into contact: the first, 'signifying', that refers to 'sensuous objects' always in excess, and that defines the edge of 'blank, mobile' desire that is 'ready to assume any contour'. . . . The second, 'signified', that refers this time to 'intellectual objects', always lacking, defining the 'obedient, conformist, plagiarizing edge'. (p. 37)

The two series made to intersect through the mana-word 'body' consist of 'word-objects' that are either overdetermined theoretically or ideologically ('intellectual objects') or underdetermined ('sensuous objects'). Such objects are produced by a 'translation into value' brought about '*at the level of the body*' (p. 21, quoting *The Pleasure of the Text*): that is, they are organized by a certain proclivity of the individual body, a 'taste or distaste', as Barthes puts it in his study of Michelet. In the signifying series of sensuous objects the 'body' is 'a place without an occupant', a '*floating signifier*' that marks each element of the series with a valence: 'I like', 'I dislike'. In the signified series of intellectual objects, the body is 'an occupant without a place,' a *floated signified* 'in search of an object or as an embryonic subject in search of an identity, or finally as a divided passive self in search of a place in the tableau of possibilities' (p. 36).

Thus the gap between the two 'edges' (*bords*) in the text (an edge that is obedient to cultural paradigms and another that transgresses them in the name of 'bliss') outlined in *The Pleasure of the Text* becomes the organizing principle of the Barthesian essay. The body is the point of their intersection (just as the narrator's body at the beginning of Balzac's *Sarrasine* effects a junction between the poles of a series of crucial antitheses: see *S/Z*, #4 seq.), but it does not abolish their heterogeneity.

On the contrary, it generates and maintains the irreducible difference that constitutes the essay as 'reflective text'.

This is not the only way to define the plurality of the essay; it can also be seen as produced by a series of 'text operators': 'evaluation, nomination, amphibology, etymology, paradox, emphasis, enumeration ...' as well as 'coupled notions' such as denotation/connotation, readerly/writerly, etc. (*Roland Barthes*, p. 92). But as Bensmaïa points out, in the selection of these operators one can discern a common principle: 'all figures will have to aid in multiplying perspectives and perpetuating the semantic duplicity that is sought. Therefore, they are all subordinated to a single one, the *figure of duplication*: double register, double thought, double band' (p. 27).

When considered from the point of view of traditional rhetorical norms, the essay can only be defined negatively. It lacks unity and continuity: it does not consist of clearly defined parts arranged in a logical order, but rather of elements apparently generated haphazardly by a more or less random, subjective association of ideas. In short, it is not *composed*. And indeed Barthes warns us that if we want to 'remain attentive to the plural of a text' we must avoid structuring it 'in large masses, as was done by classical rhetoric and by secondary-school explication' (*S/Z*, pp. 11–12).

Bensmaïa maintains that although the essay is not organized in accord with the norms of rhetorical composition (or its philosophical equivalent, systematic argumentation), it is 'nonetheless a *constituted* text on the formal plane' (p. 31). Its peculiar form of organization he calls 'procedure' (*procédé*); this includes not only the open-ended, duple structuration described above, but also 'the double resonance it introduces in the system at the level of fragments and details' as well as the effects produced by the category of 'the Neutral' (p. 51).

Barthes's predilection for the fragment can be discerned in his earliest writings, but it is first theorized and fully exploited in *S/Z* and the texts that follow it. The fragment is not, however, indivisible, atomic, the immediate constituent of the essay; on the contrary, Barthes observes that the essayistic fragment is 'subject in its very structure to asyndeton and anacoluthon, figures of interruption and short-circuiting' (*Roland Barthes*, p. 93). Bensmaïa identifies the agent of this internal division as the 'detail'. He bases his discussion of this aspect of 'procedure' primarily on Barthes's essays on cinema and photography – notably 'The third meaning' (1970) and '*Camera lucida*' (1980), where the terms 'obtuse sense' and '*punctum*' refer to details operating as an 'accentuation within the fragment' (p. 42) while remaining discontinuous with it. The *punctum* in a photograph, for instance, is a radical discontinuity that explodes within its 'obvious' (i.e. conventional) subject or meaning (the '*studium*'). The 'explosion' the detail produces within the fragment is related, of course, to what Barthes described in *The Pleasure of the Text* as 'bliss' (*jouissance*): the sudden, thrilling collapse of conventional economies of meaning that occasions a delicious 'loss of self', a *petite mort*. And like the latter, it dislocates the temporality of reading, introducing an instantaneous, vertical dimension that cuts across all forms of lexeological continuity.

The other aspect of 'procedure' outlined by Bensmaïa, which operates through the category of the 'Neutral', can also be traced back to Barthes's earliest texts. It is adumbrated in the discussion of Camus's *écriture blanche* in *Writing Degree Zero* (1954) and resurfaces in various guises from *S/Z* onward. As Barthes conceives it, 'the Neutral is not an average of active and passive; rather it is a back-and-forth, an amoral oscillation' (*Roland Barthes*, p. 132) that subverts the antinomies or oppositions on which stable meaning depends. But for the same reason it puts in question the heterogeneity of the elements that constitute the first two aspects of 'procedure', and thus 'constantly threatens to annul the infinite play of *reflection* that they command in the text' (p. 48). Hence we can say that even within the essayist's procedure itself division or discontinuity is at work.

The Neutral is not ultimately a figure of conflict, however, since the latter depends on the oppositions the Neutral subverts. As Barthes puts it, the Neutral is

> not the third term – the zero degree – of an opposition which is both semantic and conflictual; it is, *at another link of the infinite chain of language*, the second term of a new paradigm, of which violence (combat, victory, theater, arrogance) is the primary term. (*Roland Barthes*, pp. 132–3)

The Neutral thus returns as a utopian fiction, the Other of violence (of the violence of language), perhaps never to be realized but operating as a regulative ideal, an image of a future text of unlimited plurality.

The Neutral posits a difference without domination, a possibility Barthes locates in the 'phalanstery' (*Sade, Fourier, Loyola*), the seminar ('Writers, intellectuals, professors') – and the Collège de France. In his 'Inaugural Lecture,' Barthes nevertheless recognizes that the *libido dominandi* is 'hidden in any discourse, even when uttered in a place outside the bounds of power' (*Barthes Reader*, p. 459). But he insists that 'we must inquire into the conditions and processes by which discourse can be disengaged from all will-to-possess,' and adds that this inquiry 'constitutes the ultimate project' of the teaching and research he is about to undertake (ibid., p. 459). Even though *language* is inevitably linked with power, one may be able to invent a way of *performing* it in discourse that saps its inherent drive to dominate.

Barthes claims that language is 'fascist' because it not only limits what we can say, but also *compels* us to say certain things. For instance, we cannot speak for long without constituting ourselves as 'subjects' of whom certain attributes are predicated; if we speak French (or other Romance languages), we cannot easily avoid identifying ourselves as either male or female (no other options – no *neutral* or complex genders – are grammatically allowed), etc. More generally, language is both *gregarious*, in the sense that we have no choice but to use signs that exist 'only insofar as they are recognized, i.e., insofar as they are repeated' (ibid., p. 461), and immediately *assertive* (despite modal qualifications). Thus 'if we call freedom not only the capacity to escape power but also and especially the capacity to subjugate no one, then freedom can exist only outside language' (ibid.). But there is no 'outside' to language, so that its power can be resisted only through certain 'forces' within language itself, which must be exploited to 'cheat with speech, to cheat speech' (ibid.). This cheating or 'trickery' Barthes proposes to call 'literature', that is, 'the text' – or, Bensmaïa would add, 'the essay'.

If I might be permitted a digression of my own, I should say that Barthes's practice of the essay can in fact be linked to what he earlier called 'peaceable speech', ('Writers, intellectuals, professors', ibid., p. 401). One way of defining the latter would be to draw a distinction between *ironic* and *irenic* discourse. The aggressiveness of irony hardly needs stressing, and one of its more evident effects is to align the reader with the author *against* its target. Moreover, as Barthes observes in *S/Z*, ironic discourse involves (like all discourse) the repetition or quotation of another's words, but it destroys the plurality implicit in such quotation by indicating – indeed, insisting on – correct *attribution*:

> a multivalent text can carry out its basic duplicity only if it subverts the opposition between true and false, if it fails to attribute quotations (even when seeking to discredit them) to explicit authorities, if it flouts all respect for origin, paternity, propriety, if it destroys the voice which could give the text its ('organic') unity. . . . Employed in the name of a subject whose *imaginaire* is located in the distance it pretends to take with regard to the language of others, thereby making itself even more securely a subject of discourse, parody, or irony at work, is always classic language. (*S/Z*, pp. 44–5; translation modified).

An irenic discourse would seek to bracket out the signs of violence – the *libido dominandi*, the will to possess – and thus to create 'a space of discourse divested of all sense of aggressiveness' (*Barthes Reader*, p. 401). Irony is *strategic*, in so far as it assumes a sharp demarcation between *our* discursive territory and *theirs*, and aims at hegemony; Barthes's irenic discourse, condemned to operate on the enemy terrain of language, is *tactical*, 'a matter of displacing himself, obstructing . . . but not conquering', it is a 'tactics without strategy' (*Roland Barthes*, p. 172).

For Barthes, one of the attractions of such a discourse is that it is able to 'suspend or at least to delay the roles of speech – so that listening, speaking, replying, I would never be the actor of a judgment, a subjection, the advocate of a cause': to produce 'a certain dispropriation of speech' (ibid., p. 402) that is the irenic counterpart of ironic (ap)propriation. Or if there is a 'certain irony' (ibid.) in this peaceable speech, it would be precisely *uncertain*, like that of Sade, Fourier, or Flaubert, because the relation of the enunciating subject to the discourses parodied remains indeterminate (*S/Z*, p. 45).

An irenic discourse capable 'of loosening, baffling, or at the very least, of lightening' the inevitability of power in discourse would have as its fundamental operation, 'if one writes, fragmentation, and if one teaches, digression' (*Barthes Reader*, p. 476). In the 'peaceable speech' of the Barthesian essay fragmentation and digression characterize the subjects of discourse as well as its objects. Indeed, Bensmaïa suggests that as 'tactics without strategy' or as a 'novel without proper names', the essay is 'based less on the thought of *one* Author than on a "theory" of the different "postures" assumed in a necessarily *desultory* and circular manner by the presumed Author of the text as well as by the Reader' (p. 55). Discursive roles are momentarily suspended – 'everything is there, but *floating*' (*Barthes Reader*, p. 403).

The essay as reflective text 'simulates' or 'dramatizes' figures of discourse that produce plural *effects* rather than a singular meaning. It is organized in such a way that '*for every reader* there is at least one figure that cleaves him' (p. 61). The enunciating subject assumes a series of postures, in which the reader may (or may not) recognize himself ('That's it!'), and which at the same time stage alternatives, possibilities yet to be realized. Some readers may not fall for every one of these postures, but none can escape the text without being taken by at least one of them. As Barthes puts it, his text 'cruises', amorously adopting one pose after another in the hope of seducing its readers (p. 69).

The essayist's tactics are designed to address the individuality of readers – that is, of their *bodies*. For as Bensmaïa notes, from *The Pleasure of the Text* on, what most interests Barthes is the 'reader – and the writer as "lexeographer" – inasmuch as they (he) constitute(s) a particular body (of bliss): in other words, the *inexchangeable itself*' (p. 82). These essays seek to base a materialist theory of the subject on 'his' body. But this body is *plural*; Barthes is 'more and more convinced that the body proper is never anything but the fortuitous encounter of desires, of likes and dislikes, and (why not?) of contradictory Images and Phantasms that is *overdetermined socially, culturally, and historically*' (p. 83). Following Nietzsche (as read by Klossowski), he suggests that were it not for

> the *Machè* of language and the omnipotence that it despotically exercises on us, it would not be a single body – and consequently, a single 'identity' and a single 'history' once and for all – that we would be able to experience, but a multiplicity of bodies. (p. 83)

In so far as it succeeds in resisting the generalizing, 'gregarious' power of language and the hierarchies it imposes, in so far as it frees 'thought' from the domination of the 'mind' or 'soul' and restores it to the body, the essay can be said to constitute in its own way a *radical* mode of textual practice.[2]

University of Oregon

NOTES

1 *A Barthes Reader*, ed. Susan Sontag (Boston: Hill & Wang, 1982), p. 457; originally published as *Leçon* (Paris: Seuil, 1978). Subsequent references to Barthes's writings appear in the text and cite the translations published by Hill & Wang: *S/Z* (1974); *The Pleasure of the Text* (1975); *Roland Barthes* (1977).
2 I should perhaps register one caveat: as may be inferred from my discussion, Bensmaïa's book is dense, stimulating – and also very abstract. His frequent references to texts serve mainly to show that his theory of the essay can be corroborated by statements made by Barthes himself. What Bensmaïa does not offer, and what many readers will no doubt want, is an extensive examination of some of Barthes's texts to show how the structuration of the essay he describes actually operates in specific instances. It is a little as though *S/Z* were to offer its 'divagations' without the 'step-by-step' reading of Balzac's text. Now, Bensmaïa might plausibly reply that the 'divagations' are the essayistic component of *S/Z*, and that his own procedure is essayistic in that – like Montaigne and Barthes – he piles up fragments that invite further development by his readers. Whether one finds this a satisfactory reply will no doubt depend largely on one's temperament – or 'body,' as Barthes would say. In any event, Bensmaïa's seems to me clearly the best study of the formal procedures of the (Barthesian) essay currently available.

PAUL HAMILTON

● Richard Harland, *Superstructuralism* (London: Methuen, 1987), 213 pp., £5.95

Richard Harland's book begins with a bold, reductive pun, the pun of its title in which 'superstructuralism' describes both 'a larger intellectual phenomenon over and above structuralism' (p. 1), and an intellectual prerogative which inverts the usual order of Marxian base and superstructure, taking superstructure rather than base as the primary, material determinant. Harland's major structuralists (Saussure, Durkheim, Mauss, Lévi-Strauss, Jakobson, Barthes) have already set up this paradoxical convergence by postulating idealist systems ('langue', 'collective representations', 'mythologies') whose power to underwrite individual significance is experienced 'in much the same way' as the impersonal, constricting power common-sensically attributed to an external world (p. 24). The even more radical inversions of superstructuralism follow a logic of supplementarity – Althusser's 'ideology', the Foucauldian 'history of the present', Derridean grammatology, Deleuze's schizo-analysis – in which secondary, or aberrant, effects of and supposed reflections on primary material turn out not only to be presupposed by their apparent origins but also to pre-empt the materiality of these untheorized sources, 'bringing a sort of thingishness into the inside world' (p. 141). The former, structuralist materialism, according to Harland, has affinities with idealist metaphysics, and he frequently adduces parallels and contrasts with Spinoza and Hegel. Superstructuralism, although carrying a comparable metaphysical charge, eventually becomes so unrestricted in its attacks on authority as to be able to claim, paradoxically and by default, the authority of external worldliness in all its brute facticity, as it might exist prior to any theorizing, especially that required to bestow upon it its external character.

This is close to what Jay Bernstein[1] recently called, with considerable misgivings, 'a neo-Schellingian account of Derrida' – Schellingian in the sense that every signifying act is produced by an unconscious, material activity that is lost to view as soon as the differentiation it makes possible, and by which it can be recognized, supervenes. In Schelling, as in Foucault, immediate praxis can only appear as history. Harland, in his chapter on Derrida's 'general theory of Writing', similarly conceives the signifying movement productive of *différance* as taking place 'in a realm where the distinction between inside and outside no longer has any relevance' (p. 152), describable only as a 'vacuum' or 'unconscious', the traces of a materialism emptied of its logocentric history and approximating to what Derrida called in *Positions* 'radical alterity'.

Harland none the less is modest about the scope and unity of his book. He carefully limits his account to French thinkers, and keeps well away from 'the Structuralist and Post-Structuralist varieties of literary criticism' (p. 4). It is not clear how he can do this, since the absorption and reinvention of the literary to political effect within notionally autonomous disciplines is so salient a feature of poststructuralism. Metaphor and figuration do not feature in the index, and although the reading of, for instance, Derrida as a 'metaphysical materialist' is refreshingly bold and large-scale as a result, it illuminates the earlier critique of Heidegger and Husserl to the neglect of the later polemics. The absence of a rhetorical dimension to Harland's story goes with a lack of interest in the intended institutional abrasiveness or actual political domestication of the superstructuralists. For example, Kristeva, startlingly, is never discussed as a feminist. This is a likely consequence of the fact that Harland's original pun on 'superstructuralism' is taken to evoke forces which, except in the apparently unignorable case of Foucault, are not already seeking out their targets – as they clearly are for, say, Kristeva and Barthes – but, as in the case of Schelling, remain of necessity undifferentiated. Harland concedes that Kristeva and Barthes 'are original thinkers when they extend their philosophy into the field of literary criticism', and it is therefore a disappointment then to discover that 'into this field we shall not follow them' (p. 169). However, the political narrative is the book's inviting subtext, and it is worth trying to see how the common political interest reflects on the logical common denominator which Harland pursues across as wide a range of superstructuralist thinking as the space of his introduction permits.

Attempts during the last decade to produce a collaborative school of contemporary French theory tried in general to establish a working relationship between psychoanalysis, Marxism, and semiotics. Books like Coward and Ellis's *Language and Materialism* and Belsey's *Critical Practice* typically pursue a compatibility claimed to emerge when Marx is transvalued in Althusser and Macherey, semiotics is opened up to applications beyond structuralism in the deconstructive techniques of late Barthes and Derrida, and Freud is reread by Lacan. Clearly the difficulties and ingenuities involved in establishing such a canon, and the oppositional force with which its achieved unity constructs its opponents, are professionally encouraging. And in the enjoyment of the new solidarity, it is easy to overlook how selective a resumption of a wider set of possibilities it represents. What Jonathan Rée once unkindly called the *nouveau mélange* takes what shape it can more from the political credentials it seeks to establish than from unique features of technique and approach. These credentials tend to be wholesome but vague: left, anti-establishment, institutionally self-critical, keen to extract the maximum of subversive power from the disruption of internal intellectual hierarchies. In the canonical sources, though, such disruptions more openly strive to deserve the name of action, thus helping to palliate that liberal guilt at the political inefficacy of critique which is so prominent a preoccupation of the French intellectual tradition from Benda to Sartre. The new initiative contributes by supporting an attack on inherited philosophical method so radical that received procedures are best described as having been actively 'worked' on rather than revised or contradicted.

This effect, however muted its discussion in the Anglo-Saxon introductions, is arguably the most discernible one in the theories' country of origin where, as Vincent Descombes puts it, 'the relation of philosophy to *opinion* . . . is a relation primarily to *political* opinion, and secondarily to *literary* opinion'.[2] More visible there than here would be the expected, conscious donning of the mantle of that 'alterity' which repeatedly sets the limits and exposes the arbitrariness of western philosophy from Kant onwards. In the latest 'general economy' of the institution, the adoption of so openly deconstructed a position permits a much more explicit assumption of the material, working role from which past theories had always, by Marxist definition, been excluded. Contemporary interventions of so determinedly recalcitrant a kind take on the character of material displacements of traditionally idealist strongholds. Existentialist and structuralist versions of this access of authenticity are superseded by another vocabulary, simultaneously more mandarin in its negations and yet more physical in its detail than before: 'force'; 'power'; *jouissance*; *figure*; 'desiring machines'; *chora*; the dream-work that works, not thinks; all the poststructuralist resources of exorbitance, and so on. All participate in the self-targeting of reason itself: again, a process which reaches for the extra-philosophical titles of bodily activity, material practice or work the more its reflexivity and relativism advertise its procedures as noetically untenable.

However, such cultural revolutions without models (recognizably revolutionary to unprofessional 'opinion' because ambitiously unmodelled on their own discipline's criteria of coherence) may slide under yet another form of critique. They may have escaped scientificity, epistemology, and the mirror of nature only to fall captive to yet another simulation – this time, in the 'mirror of production'. Harland's book closes in a discussion of the work of Jean Baudrillard, who argues that even if that palliative of bourgeois intellectual embarrassment is realized, and theory, radically deconstructed, participates at last in its opposite categories of productive labour, a theoretical impasse is still present. It is the very notion of unalienated labour, of the immediate enjoyment of value in use, a productive creativity, that is the most successful ruse of capitalist thought. In the idea of a productivity freed of ideological representations we confront the incorrigibility of capitalism and the inescapability of philosophical tradition. For, Baudrillard claims, the political economy from whose regime Marx's solutions could not escape is nothing other than the political economy of the sign which still circumscribes the departures of the latest theoretical innovators. Authentic productivity repressively simulates labour, just as the real is a fiction as invariably motivated as the sign is arbitrary. The anthropological finality of use-value, and the sundered plenitude of the transcendental signified, are not the effective critiques of the pretensions of exchange value and discourse to possess them, but their idealist alibi. Worth and presence are so uncritically reproduced, as the 'horizon' of any act of exchange or signification, that their qualitative difference cannot disguise their uniform integration within the same economy. Thus, any deconstruction of their metaphysics only replicates their already existing position within that economy, and the truly revolutionary move would be to imagine 'symbols' not subject to it. 'Even signs must burn'.[3]

But Baudrillard's own theory must be careful not to return to being 'productive' in that Althusserian sense meant to distinguish science from ideology. He therefore tries to contrive a (still Althusserian?) grasp of the need to replace both truth and authenticity with a kind of philosophical partisanship towards a realm of 'simulation' whose universal falsity epistemology and productivity attempt to deny. As Jane Gallop neatly puts it: 'Baudrillard is writing against the history of writing against appearances.'[4] The sardonic brilliance of some of Baudrillard's examples is appealing: the ethnologists who restore the dying primitives to obscurity so that the impossible object of their science may be simulated and thus exist; or his story of how the closest apprehension of the real becomes the most synthetic – through simulacra made out of non-degradable plastics, indestructible and forever inauthentic, a kind of super-stucco or 'universal semiotic'.[5] However, the revolutionary adventures of Baudrillard's own imagination outside the political economy of the sign either take the form of *actes gratuits* or, as in *The Mirror of Production*, turn out to be Romantic tales. He avoids the Kantian aesthetic which he predictably blames for the original recuperation, as 'play', of the productivity ethic. But the 'loss' he envisages as the essence of an alternative, 'symbolic' exchange sounds once more suspiciously Schellingian. It was in art that Schelling thought we could grasp how an intelligence might lose itself in its production, figuring for him the activity of an unconscious, material Absolute, but for Baudrillard a creativity beyond the political economy of the sign; one in which the actor can abolish 'the definition of himself as labourer and the project as product of this labour' because it bears 'the inscription of the loss of finality of the subject and object'.[6]

Baudrillard's aesthetic solution might have been illuminatingly contrasted with that of Lyotard who still manages to find sufficient escape from an oppressive cultural universal or finality in defiantly local applications of the aesthetic suspension of cognitive categories after the manner of the Kantian sublime. Harland ends his superstructuralist chronology in 1976, hasn't room for Lyotard, and doesn't have much time to raise the subtext and situate Baudrillard at the end of the political road opened up by the superstructuralist paradox. The affiliations of the main characters of his narrative remain those of a strictly logical unfolding: 'the story of Superstructuralism is a story of self-purification and intensification' which 'recapitulates the Hegelian dialectic in its own trajectory' (p. 185). The repeated surfacing of a Schellingian configuration, though, suggests the movement's desire to avoid Hegelian assimilation, but at the cost of a kind of Romanticism whose materialism eludes strict idealism and everything else at the same time. Given the way Harland is forced to look for explanatory antecedents in what he calls 'Metaphysical philosophy', his argument would have been even more interesting if he had engaged with other thinkers and schools (Lukács, Adorno, Habermas?) more consciously troubled by that subreptive past. One always longs, in any case, for discussions of less well-tailored characters (Veblen, Simmel, Weber) usually bypassed on the jog which leads from Saussure to the postmodern; and it is what is interesting in Harland's book which cultivates that discontent.

Exeter College, Oxford

NOTES

1 J. M. Bernstein, *Textual Practice*, 1, 1 (Spring 1987), pp. 99–101.
2 Vincent Descombes, *Modern French Philosophy*, tr. L. Scott-Fox and J. M. Harding (Cambridge: Cambridge University Press, 1980), p. 7.
3 Jean Baudrillard, *For a Critique of the Political Economy of the Sign*, tr. with an Introduction by Charles Levin (St Louis: Telos Press, 1981), p. 163.

4 Jane Gallop, 'French theory and the seduction of feminism', in A. Jardine and Paul Smith (eds), *Men in Feminism* (London: Methuen, 1987), p. 113.
5 Jean Baudrillard, *Simulations*, tr. Paul Foss, Paul Patton, and Philip Beitchman (New York: Semiotext(e), 1983), pp. 13–18, 83–92.
6 Jean Baudrillard, *The Mirror of Production*, tr. with an Introduction by Mark Poster (St Louis: Telos Press, 1975), pp. 98–9.

K. M. NEWTON

- Stein Haugom Olsen, *The End of Literary Theory*
  (Cambridge: Cambridge University Press, 1987),
  232 pp., £25.00

Observers of the current scene in literary theory will have noticed that few of the most influential writers on the subject discuss such matters as the question of literary value or the importance of appreciating literary texts as works of art. Indeed it has been argued that literary theory should separate itself from aesthetics, and the very concept of literature as a canon of texts of aesthetic value has come under attack on a number of fronts. Terry Eagleton writes in his *Literary Theory: An Introduction*: 'The assumption that there was an unchanging object known as "art", or an isolable experience called "beauty" or the "aesthetic", was largely a product of the very alienation of art from social life which we have already touched on.' Feminist critic Dale Spender asserts in her *Mothers of the Novel*: ' "great" and "minor" are terms of which we should be highly suspicious. They are political terms.' And in *The Contest of Faculties*, Christopher Norris, writing from a deconstructionist position, attacks aesthetics as embodying right-wing ideological assumptions and argues that it is necessary to '*theorize* the mystified concepts upon which it rests'.

Stein Haugom Olsen's aim in *The End of Literary Theory* is to defend and justify literary aesthetics and to attack alternatives to it based on theories which take little or no account of aesthetics. Olsen is both a philosopher in the analytic tradition and a literary critic with publications in the field, an unusual combination. One of the interests of the book is that it is a serious attempt to use aesthetics to justify traditional literary criticism – that is, criticism of a modified New Critical type that can accommodate intentional, biographical, and historical considerations – by using various arguments of a logical and philosophical nature. In confrontations between contemporary literary theorists and supporters of traditional literary criticism, the latter have tended to resort to abuse, blanket dismissal, or easy caricature. As a result there has been little fruitful debate between contemporary theorists and traditional critics. Olsen's book makes a useful debate between the two much more likely. He presents his argument in a clear and coherent fashion, and though contemporary theorists are unlikely to agree with it, it cannot be merely dismissed as being anti-intellectual or based on ignorance of current theory. Traditional literary critics have reason to be grateful to Olsen for providing them with rational arguments which they can deploy against semoiticians, deconstructionists and other theorists.

It seems clear that aesthetics offers the most effective means for supporters of traditional literary criticism to fight back against the threat of theory. Marxists and feminists who see literature in terms of ideology or politics, or deconstructionists who reject literature as a privileged form of discourse and subsume it under textuality, are open to attack on the grounds that they have to deny that literature is constituted by aesthetic features that cannot be incorporated within political or textual categories. Olsen's defence of the latter position is vigorous and deserves the attention of anyone with an interest in aesthetics or literary theory.

Perhaps the key chapters in Olsen's book are the first and last. In the first chapter he argues that a distinction must be made between textual features and aesthetic features of literary texts, or, as he would prefer, works. All texts possess textual features which will be recognized by any linguistically competent reader but Olsen argues that aesthetic features cannot be reduced to textual terms. Aesthetic features are rather defined by the institution of literature, that is, by

> a practice whose *existence depends* both on a background of concepts and conventions which create the possibility of identifying literary works and provide a framework for appreciation, and on people actually applying these concepts and conventions in their approach to literary works. (p. 11)

Given this institutional framework underlying literary appreciation, aesthetic features cannot be dismissed as merely subjective. Olsen thus is attempting to shift the focus from literature as text to literature as a social practice in which certain conventions of reading and interpretation govern the identification of aesthetic features. Literary works are defined as those which repay the attention of those who agree to engage in this form of social practice. Though there may be disagreement about which texts should be included in the literary canon or about the interpretation of particular texts, this is not important as long as there is an agreement about the existence of a literary canon, that those texts which are part of it have cultural value, and that they respond to a certain type of interpretation: 'All the institutional theory requires to get off the ground is an agreement on what is good and what is bad argument, an agreement on which literary judgements are worth preserving and which are not' (p. 12). Since criticism should be illuminating about the literary work it can thus enhance aesthetic appreciation, and the reader's response to the literary work is 'correctly described as an *imaginative reconstruction* of its literary aesthetic features' (p. 16). He then discusses the criteria of application and the hierarchical structure of the vocabulary of literary aesthetic judgements. He describes this vocabulary as having four levels: thematic concepts; descriptive concepts; terms which connect the thematic with the descriptive; and aesthetic terms, such as balance, tension, complexity.

In his final chapter Olsen discusses literary theory's aim to offer an alternative to literary aesthetics. He had earlier argued that readers possess 'pre-theoretical intuitions' (p. 118) about how they should read literature which are a problem for advocates of systematic criticism. Here one might see a link between his position and that of Roger Scruton, whom Norris singles out for attack in *The Contest of Faculties*. Both Scruton and Olsen also have a similar view of Derrida; Olsen refers to 'the ultimate barrenness of his impenetrable jargon and the futility of an argument about texts which relies on large, unargued and less than plausible assumptions concerning the nature of language and communication' (pp. 117–18). He likewise attacks attempts at systematic theories of literature for making 'unwarranted epistemological or logical assumptions which make theory an obstacle rather than an aid in understanding the phenomenon of literature' (p. 196). He isolates three premises of literary theory which make it distinct from literary aesthetics: that (1) 'it posits a reality that is to be discovered in the text or in the relations of the text to something beyond itself'; (2) 'the reality of objects, relations, and actions posited in the metaphysical premise [i.e. the first premise] can be described or explained in a fruitful and illuminating way by help of a theoretical framework or basic method'; (3) the theory or method yields a privileged description or explanation both of the literary work and the phenomenon of literature' (p. 202). He concludes that literary theory 'represents a form of theoretical imperialism' (p. 203) which sets out to enforce acceptance and brands those who refuse to accept it as 'naïve, blind, timid, or prevented from recognizing it by some other unflattering mental weakness' (pp. 202–3). After discussing deconstruction as an example of such a systematic theory, he contrasts it with his institutional theory, which denies that a literary work can be 'defined through a set of textual features, be they relational, textural, or structural. The literary work is an irreducible entity whose literary features are grasped only in appreciation' (p. 207).

For literature to be appreciated in aesthetic terms, argues Olsen, the reader must go beyond the textual material in order to make thematic and structural connections which can imbue any particular element in a literary work with significance and interest. Such connections, he claims, do not exist at the level of the textual and can be apprehended only by a reader who understands the text as a literary work. Finally Olsen argues that a general textual theory is impossible since 'the concept of "text" is logically secondary to the concept of "work", and the concept of "work" is always a concept of a *type* of work defined by the *purposes* and *aims* the type *serves*' (p. 209). Even deconstruction is not purely textualist in approach. Olsen claims that what it does is to select certain conventions as defining literary practice, such as that literary texts possess rhetorical features, and reject others, such as that they should have artistic unity. Only if a text is understood as having a purpose beyond its textuality and is read with a knowledge of that purpose – for example, that it belongs to the 'function-category' of literature and not to that of philosophy or history – can it be properly understood.

Committed deconstructionists or semioticians will no doubt wish to take issue with Olsen's attack on theory. It seems to me, however, that the major problems are with some of his more basic assumptions. Like many philosophers writing about literature and criticism the coherence of his argument is achieved at the price of an excessive tidiness and orderliness. Literature is a messier business than he suggests and his cool style and logical approach are ill-adapted to dealing with this fact. As a result he imposes too rigid a framework on both literature and literary criticism. This can be illustrated by a comparison he makes between literary criticism and chess. In both, he claims, institutional rules govern procedures. A move in chess can be understood only if it is seen 'as contributing to the institutionally defined purpose of the game, that of attempting to win' (p. 27). But it is easy to imagine circumstances in which one may play chess, make all the correct moves, but have no intention of winning – if, for instance, one is playing against a child who would be bitterly upset at losing. I see no reason why it should be claimed that one is not playing chess in such circumstances. If I am right then one can have other purposes than the desire to win yet still be engaged in the act of playing chess. Similarly it is conceivable that readers may read literary texts with little or no interest in their aesthetic features but still have purposes which make them desire to read such texts. For example, a reader may be a philosopher whose interest is in finding philosophical significance in works of a fictional nature. Of course such an interest could be served by works which have no merit judged by literary aesthetic criteria, but I feel sure that a reader with philosophical interests would soon discover that her purposes were more likely to be served by works that were considered to be part of the literary canon. Also such a reader's interpretations of literary texts could be of considerable critical interest. There thus seems no logical reason why readers of literature who identify with the conventions governing Olsen's institution of literature should be privileged as the only authentic readers of literature.

Another example of a certain rigidity in Olsen's thinking is revealed in connection with his contention that 'It is necessary to subsume an object under a *description* in order to place it on one's conceptual map' (p. 20). To illustrate this point he asserts that if an object is classified as a stone one would expect it to possess the usual properties of stones and goes on: 'One would therefore refrain from kicking it or lifting it (if it was big), since this might result in a broken toe or a damaged spine' (p. 20). His logic does not seem to have a place for the kind of person who would be prepared to risk a broken toe in order to refute Berkeley's idealism.

One of his major claims is that only those texts which are judged to be superior because of their aesthetic features are categorized as literary and included in the literary canon. This also raises difficulties. A problem with Olsen's concept of the aesthetic is that it seems to be timeless. Yet it is clear that aesthetic features cannot be assessed in isolation from historical considerations. Many works are included in the literary canon because they happen to be historically important: they have made some stylistic or generic breakthrough, or they may be the only works of a particular period that happen to have survived. In contrast, there are works which may possess considerable aesthetic interest in terms of Olsen's concept of the aesthetic – they deal with significant themes, possess artistic unity, are written in an appropriate style – but are not part of the literary canon because they are seen as merely reproducing a past literary form, even if it could be argued that they improve on some of the earliest examples of that form. Thus a tragedy written by a modern playwright in the manner of the Jacobean dramatists is almost certain not to be included in the literary canon in spite of any aesthetic features in Olsen's sense that it may possess. Of course, if that playwright was able to convince the literary community that the tragedy was by Shakespeare it would almost certainly become part of the literary canon. Literary evaluation is not as unlike evaluation in the art market as literary critics appear to think, and it is perhaps fortunate that forgery is more difficult in literature than in painting. It is a weakness of Olsen's concept of the aesthetic that he shows little sign of appreciating these problems. It is also a pity that he does not engage directly with Paul de Man's attack on aesthetics from a theoretical standpoint in an article like 'The resistance to theory' (*Yale French Studies*, vol. 63, 1982).

Olsen is right to argue that value judgements are central to the concept of literature, but in claiming that the basis of evaluation is only aesthetic he comes dangerously close to defining literature in immanent terms: 'To understand a literary work as a literary work is thus to understand how its properties (the identification of which are made possible by the institution of literature) contribute to aesthetic value' (p. 24). There are a number of evaluative criteria that can result in texts being placed within the literary canon, not only aesthetic but historical, political, social, philosophical, to name the most obvious, or combinations of these. It is likely that the power of feminism as an ideology will lead to certain texts that are open to a strong feminist interpretation being included in the canon even though they may have been judged previously as weak in aesthetic terms. Another important consideration is that the purpose of having a literary canon, that is, a limited number of works believed to possess special merit, only makes sense because life is short and there is not an unlimited amount of time to engage in reading. The reader with literary interests will want to select those texts which seem most worthy of attention, and the canon helps one in this selection process. But various compromises govern inclusion in the canon: the stylistic innovation of one work competes with the thematic complexity or historical importance of another work. Different eras will have different priorities and this will lead to changes in the canon. It is also unlikely that readers with literary interests will confine their reading to the official canon but will seek out marginal or non-canonic texts which they find of greater literary interest than certain texts which are regarded as canonic.

Olsen does not discuss John M. Ellis's definition of literature in his book *The Theory of Literary Criticism* – indeed, this book is a notable omission from Olsen's bibliography. Ellis argues that texts categorized as literary possess no immanent characteristics. Literature, he concludes, can be defined only as linguistic products which the community decides to use in a certain way. This definition, which avoids the claim that literary value is to be identified with aesthetic features, seems to raise fewer problems than Olsen's definition.

One of Olsen's most provocative chapters is entitled 'On unilluminating criticism'. Here he contests the claims of any theory governed by assumptions that cannot be reconciled with his institutional framework for criticism. He argues that Harold Bloom's interpretation of Blake's 'London' in *Poetry and Repression* involves accepting ideas that are so idiosyncratic and information that is so remote from the poem that, however imaginative Bloom's reading may be, it does not aid appreciation. But are Bloom's assumptions as unacceptable as Olsen makes out? Bloom only demands that one accept the Freudian concept of repression and that poetry should be seen as exploiting the sources of words for its effects as well as the words themselves. Even if the reader does not go all the way with Bloom's poetic theory, it has the benefit from the reader's point of view of allowing a poem which previously had been caught up in the vice-like grip of previous interpretative approaches to exist in a new mental space and thus to acquire new life.

Olsen's negative response to Bloom and other forms of theoretical criticism, such as deconstruction, is not unconnected with the fact that his aesthetics of literary appreciation operates as a largely passive contemplation of a text's artistic unity. One's doubt about this concept of literary aesthetics is whether it can meet the challenge of aesthetic theories which see art as disrupting ordering categories or demanding an active relation between the work of art and its perceiver/interpreter. Olsen does not discuss the aesthetics of critical theories which see literature as undermining formal expectations of order, such as Russian Formalism with its concept of defamiliarization, or which conceive of the reader–text relation as interactive, such as those forms of phenomenological criticism which argue that the reader must fill in gaps or blanks in the text.

A major underlying issue of Olsen's book concerns the teaching of literature. Somewhat unfashionably he has confidence that teaching literature in terms of literary aesthetics is at least as valid as a means of training the mind and the sensibility as the teaching of, say, philosophy or science. One feels that a significant proportion of teachers of literature in higher education have lost such confidence. Thus it is argued that one should not be teaching literature in any canonic sense but textuality or literature as part of cultural history alongside other texts on an equal footing. Whether this shift is based on a belief that such approaches are more worthwhile educationally than an aesthetically based approach, or on an opportunistic attempt to prevent literature being outflanked by media studies, or on a resigned acceptance of a situation in which students, because of a cultural resistance to reading, inadequate educational background and so on, are just incapable of responding to writing in aesthetic terms, is a matter open to debate. In defending literary aesthetics and attacking the adequacy of theoretical alternatives Olsen raises important educational questions which are of concern to all teachers of literature. This adds to the value of what is already a challenging and consistently interesting book, though some readers, accustomed to a more flamboyant approach to literary theory, may find that its dry, analytic style takes some adjusting to.

University of Dundee

ALAN DURANT

- Richard Leppert and Susan McClary (eds), *Music and Society: the Politics of Composition, Performance and Reception* (Cambridge: Cambridge University Press, 1987), 202 pp., £25.00

Among cultural forms whose production, reception, and interpretation have been studied using recent techniques of cultural analysis, music has remained a sleeping partner. While the study of film, television, literature and non-literary discourse has been scrutinized, revolutionized, and re-institutionalized by successive new approaches relating aspects of form to considerations of meaning and social context, the study of music has remained dominated by two generally unconnected, older paradigms:

1 the concern in traditional musicology with form as an 'autonomous' level of artistic expression, crowned with an almost mystical aura of sensitivity and achievement. This is a concern with musical form to the virtual exclusion of the social context in which it was devised or the various social contexts in which it has been consumed – a concern

which continues, in an inflected form, in contemporary work on music perception influenced by generative grammar and cognitive science.

2 the concern in modern cultural studies with music as one defining element of subculture and with sociological questions of the production, representation, and consumption of different kinds of music. (These studies differ methodologically from, but nevertheless retain some degree of common cause with, traditional music history. After accumulating and structuring contextual material they frequently say in effect: now see for yourself how this contextualization of the music affects your listening.) Such investigations are by and large all context, with little or no capacity to say much of interest about form or the way it contributes to pleasure or interpretation.

Alongside and between these two traditions, however, there are alternative, less established lines of musicological argument. These stretch from Adorno, Benjamin and Eisler, through Barthes and Nattiez, into contemporary work by Attali and others, and are unified by a common concern to speculate on relations between musical forms, the ways they create pleasures and 'meanings', and the larger technological, economic, and ideological formations in which they serve a function.

The collection of essays *Music and Society: The Politics of Composition, Performance and Reception* marks an attempt to consolidate these approaches – and build on from them – into what would be in effect a manifesto of new musical studies. Made up of reworked papers initially given at a conference held at the University of Minnesota in 1985, the collection promises to introduce musicologists and music students previously sheltered by the academic horizons of their discipline from critical work on music and society – as well as from recent theoretical work in adjacent fields (such as literary theory, social theory, and psychoanalysis) – to a set of issues which indicate collectively an alternative, politically and educationally polemical, direction for future work in the study of music.

Three main purposes emerge. First, *Music and Society* aims to force together studies of musical form (its 'syntax', or rhythmic, harmonic, and textural structures) with questions of social and historical context (such as those surrounding biography, patronage, circumstances of performance, etc.). Second, the book is to undermine the current academic primacy of the established musical canon, and set the study of currently marginalized musics (the introduction identifies musics by western women and ethnic and racial minorities, as well as non-western musics) on an equal methodological footing with study of the canon. Third, the book seeks to expose the way in which pleasure in music comes from what is suggested to be a listener's withdrawal into an imaginary realm detached from political and social realities. Recognizing the escapist character of this type of pleasure is taken to be a necessary first step towards getting politics back into listening. This restructuring of pleasure is then thought capable of undermining our appearance to ourselves as unified *subjec-*

tivities responding to music. At the same time, with the dispersal of the mystical 'aura' of art into the contradictions of material existence, music would be granted 'both the powers and the responsibilities of a genuinely political medium' (p. xix).

These aims, which are usefully outlined in the Introduction, are recognizable: together, they are to link up musicology with modern work in literary and social theory. In fact, to anyone coming to the book with a familiarity with 'theory', the dependence on priorities and positions in these fields will be frequently apparent (not only in the ways issues are discussed but also in the unquestioned assumption – difficult for readers coming from traditional musicology – of the importance and broader, 'strategic' political usefulness of this sort of work). But beyond the application of existing theoretical frameworks to musical case studies (which is undoubtedly useful for musicology), the more interesting question becomes: does *Music and Society* show up anything specific about music in relation to this theoretical orientation, or is the new sound of music studies simply the transposition of theory's radical tunes into a new key, for a new audience?

Most of the essays in the collection, unfortunately, are not as interesting as the broad canvas of the Introduction and the book's attractive subtitle – 'the politics of composition, performance and reception' – seem to promise. In fact, the editors' Introduction is possibly the most useful part of the book, laying out directions the study of music should pursue in a checklist of issues which could be usefully read by anyone starting out on musicological research or curriculum development. Disappointingly, though, the Introduction gets increasingly entangled in trying to show, against the odds, how each of the various, very different chapters which follow contributes to these aims.

'Against the odds', because the papers themselves are a very uneven collection. Immediately after the editors' Introduction comes a chapter by Janet Wolff which spells out the arguments against seeing art as an autonomous practice or body of artefacts disconnected from surrounding social circumstances. This will serve as a useful primer for anyone coming to the idea cold, and contains a good account of the emergence of Romantic ideas of the artist, but is damaged by virtually exclusive use of examples from arts other than music, followed by the unsupported assertion that despite its non-representational character, music 'does not present any special problems' as regards forms of analysis which combine semiological and sociological perspectives.

The remaining chapters – which might put this idea to the test – leave, at least to my mind, that claim fairly much up in the air. Three chapters, for example, simply push what are initially good ideas too far and in unhelpful directions.

Richard Leppert's own chapter, 'Music, domestic life and cultural chauvinism: images of British subjects at home in India', starts with the interesting idea of studying the conflict between eighteenth-century ideas of nature-inspired 'harmony' as a structuring, rational principle of art and the manifest social inequalities of British colonialism, by looking at paintings done in colonial India which show musical instruments. All that is shown, though, is the obvious: that images of musical instruments in paintings (in this case, western instruments) are deployed, like images of everything else, within networks of conventions governing symbolic interpretation (cf. the hearth, the globe, or landscaped parks) which endorse socially prevailing, often reactionary ideologies – in this instance, those of imperialism.

John Shepherd's chapter on 'Music and male hegemony' starts from the idea that the visual arts are fetishistic and controlling, and so support male hegemony, whilst the relation of musical sound to the uncloseable ear opens up radical potentialities: 'the very fact of music, based as it is on the physical phenomenon of sound, constitutes a serious threat to the visually mediated hegemony of scribal elites' (p. 157). Shepherd then improvises around the idea that timbre may be the primary, physiological determinant of musical politics, but without ever presenting or referring to evidence or explanation that might lead anyone to believe this – effectively trivializing the important issues of gender that the chapter promises to consider.

The category of a 'structure of listening' is introduced by John Mowitt, in an argument which – drawing more on Walter Benjamin's discussions of 'aura' than on Raymond Williams's 'structure of feeling' – hopes to show finally 'the emancipatory dialectic of contemporary musical reception'. This is an enticing possibility, until the radical future for listening turns out to be no more than freely metaphorical speculation around the binary character of the 'bit' as the organizing principle of digital technology: radical musical aspirations become merely waiting for a time when 'the frayed fabric of tradition will be rewoven with optical fibers and the conditions for auratic reception will be restored' (p. 193).

Fortunately, these three chapters don't provide the only flavour of the collection. Two papers – which seem to me central to *Music and Society*'s project – do seek to interconnect contextual factors with questions of musical form and interpretation in more rigorous ways.

'On grounding Chopin' comes at the problem by seeking to show that forms have a material history (of innovation, circulation, prestige, etc.) which provides a resource for allusion and influence that fixes notions of 'autonomous', abstract form in historically specific patterns of affiliation and reference. Rose Rosengard Subotnik goes on in this chapter to suggest that serious consideration of Chopin's style necessitates investigation of such issues. This might seem a bottom-drawer lecture on 'how much of a Romantic was Chopin' rewritten to fit the themes of the conference except that the Chopin argument is embedded primarily as exemplification in the larger argument detailing interconnections between history and formal interpretation.

Similarly, in 'The blasphemy of talking politics during Bach Year', Susan McClary uses analogous arguments about the historical materiality of Bach's musical styles to probe the current issue of the myths of creativity and divine inspiration which surround Bach's work. Such arguments are convincing and important. Unfortunately, though, in later stages of the paper they get hooked into larger historical speculations which seek to tie the knot on evident links between the history of tonal music and the rise and decline of the European bourgeoisie. The periodization seems right, the analogies with capitalism, the subject in law, perspective drawing and the iambic pentameter are all in place; all that remains is to fit tonality into the pattern. But there's a problem: tonality in McClary's argument simultaneously articulates social values 'held most dear by the middle class: beliefs in progress, in expansion, in the ability to attain ultimate goals through rational striving . . .' and yet also has ascribed to it a 'destabilising, exuberant, subversive character', resisted by musical establishments (p. 22). So the third, and most grand, level of argument falters – but it leaves the detailed Bach analysis and the demystification of Bach Year among the best sections of the collection.

Beyond what's in the various chapters, though, there is also the question – especially given the aspiration of the book to be a major 'place marker' in the discipline – of the selection of topics for inclusion. Most of the chapters are either directly or indirectly about the European concert tradition, even if they are seeking to deconstruct it; and in this respect, *Music and Society* doesn't to my mind problematize the social and educational standing of that canon adequately. As with critical work deconstructing the literary canon, one issue too often neglected is the extent to which these deconstructions are of a genuinely ideologically dominant cultural force as against the extent to which they address a specialist cultural interest which increasingly grips an academic minority far more than it grips anyone else – a cultural force in the process for the larger public of being reshaped, gradually marginalized, even bypassed, by changing patterns of cultural production and consumption which have no place in deconstruction's brief.

There is a great deal which needs to be said on all sides of this issue, which raises fundamental questions about the 'strategic' value of – and directions for – critical work. Given its importance, however, the single chapter which considers such questions (by Simon Frith, laying out a framework for an aesthetic of popular music) seems almost tokenistic. Frith's argument is that since different codes of evaluation are applied to 'serious' music and to 'popular' music, the task of relating music to society will be different for each. For serious music, widely revered as transcendent and formally autonomous, the task is that of showing music's dependence on specific social circumstances; for popular music, on the other hand, widely dismissed as being exhaustively determined and limited by its social function, the task is that of taking seriously the usually disregarded aesthetic values which surround it. From this starting-point, Frith goes on to analyse the myth of 'authenticity' in popular music, and describes an aesthetic of popular music located in different kinds of *construction*, rather than in representations, of images of authentic identity. Finally, in an important commentary on this description, Frith spotlights the necessary questions of politics and value that any consideration of popular music raises. These are precisely the questions it becomes difficult to address – but which it is nevertheless imperative to tackle – when the bridge of anthropological self-scrutiny has been crossed, the deconstruction of the canon set in process, and all musics actually begin to be considered (as *Music and Society* proposes they should be) on an equal methodological footing.

Music and Society evidently aims to be a turning-point in the study of music and, given the range of currently available sources in musicology, it is likely to prove a useful reference point. Certainly there is a need to break down consideration of 'music' into analysis of different genres, and to connect the formal features of these genres (such as harmonic and rhythmic structure, texture, use of voice, combination with rhetorics of image in performance, etc.) with changing social and historical contexts and forces. These include patterns of relative prestige between different kinds of music, the unequal relationships of power and control which surround performance and music distribution, and the contexts – and economic and technological conditions – in which various kinds of music are produced and consumed. Neither playing nor listening to music takes place in a vacuum, and so historicized, contextualized studies of composition, performance, and reception are urgently needed.

The importance of *Music and Society* is its clear concern to contextualize analysis and interpretation, and to dislodge the academic hold of the classical concert repertoire – so enabling musicology to draw alongside contemporary literary and media studies. The danger of this parity between the study of music and other areas of cultural studies being achieved through widespread use of this collection in particular, though, is that readers may confuse the real value of raising the questions *Music and Society* raises with the much lesser value of the particular steps towards answers the book offers.

University of Strathclyde

STEPHEN BYGRAVE

- Imre Salusinszky, *Criticism in Society: Interviews with Jacques Derrida, Northrop Frye, Harold Bloom, Geoffrey Hartman, Frank Kermode, Edward Said, Barbara Johnson, Frank Lentricchia, and J. Hillis Miller* (New York and London: Methuen, 1987), 244 pp., £17.95 (hardback), £5.95 (paperback)
- Robert Moynihan, *A Recent Imagining: Interviews with Harold Bloom, Geoffrey Hartman, J. Hillis Miller, Paul De Man* (Hamden, Conn.: Archon Books, 1986), 168 pp., $17.50

In another review of the Salusinszky volume Chris Baldick wrote that literary theory now had its very own hardcover fanzine. You see what he means, even though the review editor of *Textual Practice* has only run to the paperback for me. For instance we learn from one of the interviews with Harold Bloom (though not the other) that he calls everyone 'my dear', and J. Hillis Miller has a good story about the first time Bloom saw a cow ('*What* is *that enormous* hairy animal?'). There are some good jokes and there's some good fun – Hillis Miller again, the last of Salusinszky's interviewees, triumphantly caps readings of a poem proffered by those earlier in the series, and claims a pioneer spirit in his imminent translation to an endowed chair at Irvine: 'Twenty years ago it was just a cow-pasture; twenty years from now it may be a cow-pasture again.' Paul de Man is quite willing to play Morris Zapp, courteously answering Moynihan's request for a definition of deconstruction with a single sentence and even offering a slogan for a lapel-badge: 'There is no valid text, but some invalid texts are more validly invalid than others!' Well, maybe it would have to be a T-shirt. Northrop Frye, who's interviewed in the Salusinszky volume, writes somewhere that myth is gossip grown old. With the exception of Bloom's myth-making the contemporary gossip here is from interviewees who are unpretentious and relaxed – off-guard even. Moynihan's blurb promises that 'all who are seriously interested in literature, literary theory, and intellectual life generally will have a lot of fun with this book.' His interviews with the Yale Fab Four were conducted between 1979 and 1985. Three of them are also interviewed by Salusinszky, who taped a total of nine interviews in 1985 and 1986 – a pluralism which allows in two Europeans, and one woman.

The two books have other similarities: they use the same photos of the three critics they duplicate, courtesy of the Yale University Office of

Public Information. (If this reviewer were not 'seriously interested . . . etc.' he'd have wished that Methuen had used the author's photograph from the back of *Agon*, snapped, if he remembers rightly, by a – presumably vengeful – Mrs Bloom.) Both volumes take one paradigm of 'criticism in society' from the Cambridge English Faculty ruckus of 1981, on which the saddest and wisest, though most guarded, comments are from Frank Kermode, who was there; Moynihan's book has a title and an epigraph from Wallace Stevens and Salusinszky's plan was for each of his critics to show the folks how they would read the same Stevens poem (differently, was the hope), thereby participating in what he calls a 'seminar of the air'. It's no surprise that this doesn't work very well and often breaks down. (It's a bit like the enterprise of another book I was sent for review in which critics offered various kinds of reading of three or four short texts – structuralist, Lacanian, Marxist, and so on: an approach which a friend of mine likened to trying on funny hats.) At one point Kermode and Salusinszky have both forgotten to bring their copies of the poem, and instead Kermode presents his interlocutor with an obscene acrostic.

Understandably shy of adding to the pile of honourable verbiage headed 'The Function of Criticism' from which he quotes in his introduction, Salusinszky plays the *ingénue*: 'since the best thing to do with one's obsessions is always to foist them upon unwilling strangers, it seemed a good time to go around and put questions about the function of criticism to people who might be expected to provide some interesting answers'. Actually his book implies a genealogy very similar to that in Frank Lentricchia's *After the New Criticism*, begotten by Frye out of Stevens. Thus the first interview, with Jacques Derrida, stands rather apart from the others: Derrida features as an unbuttoned entrepreneur with novelistic ambitions and is not given a seat in the aerial seminar-room. Frye too is rather reverently treated in an interview understandably much more retrospective than the others. His interviewer's only flash of scepticism occurs when Frye makes optimistic noises about the prospects for humanities in the academy due to his 'realisation that everything does go in cycles'. Elsewhere Salusinszky's interviewing persona is engagingly reminiscent of Basil Fawlty explaining away Manuel ('I'm not a threat: I'm from Australia'), but its skill should not be underrated. Moynihan's interviewing technique is more often to ask questions along the lines of 'What do you mean by . . . ?' In his interview with Bloom they're discussing Arnold and there's this exchange:

> *Do you think the snobbery of the English class system was an impediment for Arnold?*
> Oh, I dare say that it was, but I'm not much given to social analysis of literary matters.

And so back to Arnold's poetry. In Salusinszky's corresponding interview he elicits this from a much more hyped-up Bloom: 'The poet is not a slum-lord; the critic is not a hireling of the stock exchange. I am weary of this nonsense, and will not put up with it.' Mischievously, he later quotes this to Frank Lentricchia, which leads to some of the best pages in the book.

Salusinszky's interview with Bloom is a comic *tour de force*, and despite the way that, as Hillis Miller puts it, 'the assemblage you have and some of the things that are said – including by you – . . . give Frye . . . centrality, as our father', Bloom is the real star here and not merely the comic relief. All the other interviewees adopt positions opposed to the devil's advocacy of Bloom that 'there is no social dimension to what we do. . . . Reading, teaching, being taught: the experience of literature is the experience of an isolate and solipsizing glory.' Bloom offers this as 'just pragmatic' and it has to be said that some of the opposed versions here of 'reading, teaching, being taught' could easily be disparaged with one or other of his favourite terms – 'idealizing' or 'positivist'. For instance, what probably sounded fair enough when Barbara Johnson said it may look embarrassingly smug to her in print:

> You could say that this institution is not going to be substantially changed by me, or by anything that I do, enough to cease to be influential in shaping people who will probably become leaders in this country. Therefore, how should I contribute to the training of leaders in this country, to bring about a better understanding on their part of justice, or reading, or whatever you want to call it? This certainly seems to be what I tend to do, but I'm glad that there are people who think that more drastic measures are needed. It just seems like that's what I'm equipped to do.

If this sounds like the familiar rationalization of a liberal dilemma we should remember where we are: Salusinszky stresses that 'the purview of the book is North American' – actually almost exclusively the United States where, as I write, the outgoing President has told his party to go ahead and use 'the L-word' for the policies of the Democratic candidate. Not much that is flattering is said about British academe, especially by the lone Briton, though there is some talk about the way Marxism has always been treated seriously here and some envy of our 'socialist tradition'. The interview with Hartman in the Moynihan volume expresses admiration for the European intellectual who can combine writing with political activism (for Malraux and even Mitterand as well as for Sartre) and it concludes with a discussion of Hartman's involvement in the protests against Reagan's visit to the cemetery at Bitburg.

Among other things that this might be connected to is Hartman's suspicion of demystification as an urge for purification which can go totalitarian. He wants to retain the play of what he calls enchantment – in criticism as well as literature. For the 'worldly' or 'secular' critics in the second half of the volume the retention of mystery is an effort to shore up a priestly caste, a form of the authority with which the texts they teach are imbricated. Moynihan's interviews with Bloom and Hartman are much occupied with the state of Judaism in the United States and with the agenda for a recovery of its study in the academy. On one level of course this is an argument about the canon and the syllabus. There is another argument however. Salusinszky's interviewees variously reject Frye's (or for that matter Abrams') notion of English Romanticism as a displacement of Protestant myth, and this raises ideological as well as administrative problems about what is to replace it. Hartman speaks of having 'taught ... students Christianity by teaching them Spenser' at post-war Yale where, he says, anti-semitism was institutionalized. It would be interesting to know, in this connection, how they've reacted to the news about the early publications de Man omitted from his CV. Hartman, who was a refugee from Nazi Germany and is, I think, in charge of Yale's archive of Holocaust material, is much surer talking about the Bitburg issue than he is talking about the academic institution. All the interviewees talk about 'reading, teaching, being taught' as transitive activities (even where, in Bloom's case, 'poetry does not teach us to talk to other people: it teaches us how to talk to ourselves'). Given this – and given too that Salusinszky's interviewees were each shown transcripts of the earlier interviews – we start wishing for an extension of the interview formula to debate focused on issues other than the poem. There is of course something ridiculous in the wish – perhaps each should have been sent something like a market-research form? – but the wish is prompted by the sense that sometimes Salusinszky's very tact as an interviewer can stifle debate. For example, the term 'Zionism' crops up repeatedly in his interview with Edward Said, once with reference to Bloom and Hartman, but it's never used when he interviews them. There is a point in Moynihan's interview with him where Bloom's refusal of what Said would call the worldliness of criticism can seem less amusing. When Moynihan probes him on Israeli politics Bloom replies 'Who can be upset? One just wants Israel to survive.' Next question.

Salusinszky remarks of his interviews that in them the 'religious' critics are succeeded by the 'secular'. (If the structure of his volume is, thus, redemptive, what does that make Hillis Miller?) It's certainly the case that for the later interviewees self-consciousness about the activities of 'reading, teaching, being taught' does not take the form of positing possible determinants of those activities as an 'other'. It will come as a surprise to some that Jacques Derrida uses the word 'apocalypse' in much the same way as it's used in the newspapers, as opposed to the way it's used transcendentally by, say, Hartman. Salusinszky's interviews with Said, Johnson and Lentricchia are exemplarily fascinating texts in their own right, as is Moynihan's with de Man. Lentricchia comes on with an attractive, let's-cut-the-crap attitude not dissimilar to Bloom's. Though his justification for what he's doing in academe – 'there is no greater opportunity than the opportunity of perverting the young' – is simply a tougher-sounding version of Johnson's formulation, it's with Lentricchia's impatience of certain political claims made for deconstruction that we can end:

It may be very true that authority stands on an abyss, but in the meanwhile the woman at the A & P is making two dollars an hour and has six kids to feed, and her boss doesn't know that the authority of his rhetoric stands on an abyss and probably wouldn't give a shit if one of us told him so.

Again, next question.

King's College, London

EDMOND WRIGHT

- Dalia Judovitz, *Subjectivity and Representation in Descartes: The Origins of Modernity* (Cambridge: Cambridge University Press, 1988), 230 pp., £25.00
- Seppo Sajama and Matti Kamppinen, *A Historical Introduction to Phenomenology* (London: Croom Helm, 1987), 131 pp., £18.95 (hardback), £8.95 (paperback)

Alexander Bryan Johnson, the nineteenth-century American linguist, can be looked upon as a robust anti-Cartesian. On the cover of the Dover edition of his *Treatise on Language* is what purports to be a photograph of him: there is also a photograph of him as a frontispiece to the book. However, one is obviously a mirror-image of the other, a fact that would have amused Johnson himself. Which is the true photograph of the author? We have no idea, yet according to the 'clear and distinct' canons of logic it must be true that one photograph is of Johnson and one is not of Johnson. Suppose that only one had been used, the false one: would it have been of no use? Not at all, for it would have given a sufficient likeness of him for us to recognize representations of him again.

We are more acquainted with the false image we get of ourselves in a mirror than what we really look like, and yet we call it 'me' without any qualms, as free from doubt as Descartes himself uttering the *cogito*. Whether the entity singled out from reality be an object like a photograph or a subject such as oneself, it is obvious that neither yield with ease to a simple true/false analysis. If we aim to be 'masters and possessors of nature', a phrase of Descartes's that Dalia Judovitz usefully singles out for us, we are likely to meet with disappointments, especially if we rely too readily upon unquestioned certainties. If we go further and expect them to fit timelessly under given quantifications, we are more likely to find nature the mistress.

Dalia Judovitz's excellent attack on Cartesianism is particularly welcome at a time when the dinosaur is still asserting its anachronistic presence in more than one discipline. She has worked on the principle that there must be 'a strategic and necessary juncture' of the philosophical, literary, and artistic domains: typically her own strategy has been to make a philosophical critique via an analysis of Descartes's own rhetoric. This allows her to cross the academic frontier, not with naïve temerity, but with a formidable thrust.

In Descartes's continued meditations upon the Self she is able to point to the glaring inconsistency – one that amounts to deception of self and reader – between the would-be autobiographical style and the anonymity of that concept of the Self he is at pains to foist upon us. She brings out the irony of a fragment of a life-story which endeavours to move outside the idea of a fiction. In one moment we seem to be with the real-life Descartes, sitting beside a fire, the next moment we are faced with a disembodied transcendental subject whose only claim to reality is an intuition based upon the single thought of existence. We who are now wisely suspicious of authors who claim to know all about their utterances are not going to be so easily imposed upon. In order to get beyond the linguistic conventionality of the use of 'I' in the *Cogito, ergo sum* of the *Discours* or the 'I am, I exist' of the *Meditations*, we have to explore the context in which we find them, since we no longer have the living speaker before us with whom to negotiate. Such an exploration is precisely Judovitz's successful method.

Descartes is telling a fiction, she says, at the very moment he is ostensibly rejecting it. Indeed, he follows Plato's own suspicion of fiction, and for the same reason, yet it is in that very rejection that both of them reveal their bewitchment. Judovitz notes that fiction is the 'ultimate form of alienation' for Descartes; only mathematics can give the familiarity of being absolutely certain: 'Outre que les fables font imaginer plusieurs événements comme possibles qui ne le sont point.' (Fables make one imagine many events possible which in reality are not so.) (Judovitz, p. 100).

It is worthwhile trying to see this as funny, something one can do with many of Descartes's po-faced dicta. The computer-software expert Emmanuel Lehman has recently said that we cannot depend upon the concepts with which we are currently operating, because, such being the infinitude of the continuum and the complexity of nature, we can never be sure that we have all understood our 'discretizing' the same way.[1] If that is the case, then our current concepts partake of the nature of fables to a degree we cannot at present determine: they are mutual postulates, so far successful and no more. So all our empirical concepts (including our self-concept) that we 'take to be true' are to some degree 'fables' – they 'make us imagine many events possible that are not so'. Descartes deconstructs himself.

Judovitz brings out another fatal consequence of this ignoring of the empirical self, namely, that it automatically inhibits Descartes and anyone else following the Cartesian line from inquiring into the genesis of the Self. The senses and the memory are seen with Plato as only 'fluctuating testimony', though Descartes had to admit in the *Meditiations* that memory did provide the only sure foundation for distinguishing between waking and sleep. The ego, on the other hand, is taken as a self-created entity, one that, on the firm foundations that self-certainty and mathematics provide, can freely explore the logical architecture of the universe. Judovitz quotes Descartes as preferring those buildings where a single architect has had the freedom to pursue his own style regardless of pre-existing tradition or, presumably, anyone else's preferences. The only way in which Descartes can conceive of a threat to his self-certitude is significantly in his fiction of an evil genius that could be fooling him completely, a dream which, one cannot but acknowledge, has a quite paranoid character. Truth and fiction are fearfully to be kept in separate compartments. Judovitz is nevertheless able to show that Descartes was unconsciously borrowing from discussions of illusion in contemporary French fiction: the question 'How do I know I am not dreaming?' had already been raised and explored in a novel by Honoré D'Urfé.

Judovitz points out that modernism is inextricably linked with this same fearfulness. The true artist, to be worthy of the modernist definition, has had to project himself as a 'supreme and sovereign subjectivity'. He projects an order outwards solely from private intuitions, discontinuous with all traditions (p. 195). Science, too, must have nothing to do with art, and, in particular, investigations into rhetoric are to be ruled out. Judovitz returns us healthily to Montaigne, whom she regards as postmodern in his challenging of the bounds of conceptual and aesthetic domains (p. 194). Better 'Que sais-je?' than 'Je pense, donc je suis.'

Central to the whole question of conceptualization is that of representation. If a mathematical discourse is going to have a foundational certainty then the order of the mental representation will be taken to be the order of things. Descartes does concede that experiment is necessary, but this goes along with the belief that a completed physics will be a through-and-through axiomatic system. His aim is to transform all things into mathematical signs, which amounts to a blatant 'downgrading of experience' (p. 48).

The same urge to match representation and reality is present in the phenomenologists and the philosophers who are their forebears. Though Husserl talked of 'suspending' the natural attitude and not of doubting it, there is the same Cartesian desire to establish certain foundations for knowledge. His 'epoche' is basically the same philosophical Platonist move, a temporary retreat from engagement with sentient experience in search of an abstract validity. He hoped to arrive at the essences of things by an inner intuition, where transcendental object and transcendental self would confront each other in 'eidetic purity'. To be fair to Husserl, his later work, particularly *Experience and Judgement*, does not share the same fervour for such verities as his earlier *Logical Investigations* and *Ideas*.

Sajama and Kamppinen's book sets out to be an outline guide to the historical origins of phenomenology, and in this regard it succeeds admirably. Any undergraduate student, not only of phenomenology but of the origins of linguistic philosophy, would be well advised to purchase it. It has the great merit of pedagogical clarity, often illustrating arguments with helpful diagrams and pursuing the intricacies of the relationships of one argument with another without confusion. The book originally arose out of a series of lectures which the authors modestly say were 'haphazard' in character, but there is nothing haphazard about the present book. It deals in turn with the Object Theory of knowledge and representation, as evidenced by Reid, Brentano, and the earlier Meinong, and the Content Theory, whose exemplars were the later Meinong and Husserl. It also includes discussions of Husserl's notions of 'adumbration' and 'horizon', the problem of *de re* and *de dicto* acts, and the intentionality of emotions. The authors make no bones about their own commitments, which is a good thing, coming out plainly with carefully argued cases in most chapters for their espousal of the Content Theory.

Briefly, the Object Theory characterizes all intentionality, and hence all conscious mental phenomena, as directed toward an object which, in Brentano's view, is intramental. A judgement is made about a particular on the basis of a 'presentation', and it can be judged to exist or to be imaginary. Note the Cartesian obsession with keeping 'objects' and 'fictions' apart. It is significant that so many of the philosophers falling within the historical and thematic scope of this book are deeply concerned to find rational homes for 'centaurs' and 'golden mountains' as well as the illusions of those who take the Morning Star to be a different entity from the Evening Star. Sajama and Kamppinen can easily trip Brentano up, because his own desire to get consciousness as atomistically ordered as physics led him into confusions about whether he meant presentations to be epistemically neutral or to embody conceptual content.

Meinong is the philosopher whom the hard-headed realists of today can find so Byzantine because his ontology includes the golden mountain, admittedly all on different 'levels of being' from, say, Searle's glass on the table. What has been forgotten by Sajama and Kamppinen is that he was trying to account for the intentional side of perception, and, if one accepts that existence is apprehended through presentations, it is not impossible to have abnormalities occurring in them, for they would be part of an empirical system. If a computer throws randomized patterns on a TV screen and one of them happens by chance to resemble a glass of water, did you or did you not see a glass of water? For didn't the glass of water exist in some sense or other?

Sajama and Kamppinen present the Content Theory, whether in Frege's version of 'Expression-Sense-Reference' or Husserl's of 'Act-Content-Object', as endeavouring to account for the subject's part in singling out objects from nature by inserting a reliable identifying device between the Act and the Object. Frege was determined to make his 'sense' a public affair, one common across persons. Like Husserl he was at pains to avoid the accusation of 'psychologism', the suggestion that judgements about object-existence could be based on something as private and uncheckable as one man's subjective experiences. This he believed would plunge scientific certainty into the abyss of relativism. Similarly, Husserl's *noema* was on the ideal level, bestowing the certainty that the private encounter with the sensory base, the 'hyle', could not.

It is here that Sajama and Kamppinen come up to date, say, with the contemporary phenomenologist David Woodruff Smith, who holds with Husserl that there is one thing that bestows the certainty of objects, even – and we expect this to be said – across illusions.[2] They point out that Husserl admitted that percepts could 'explode', as when what one takes to be a man turns out to be a mannequin. What saves the day, they claim, is Husserl's 'determinable X', the single unique entity that is preserved as the core of reference across the two gestalts, man to mannequin. But Husserl forgot that gestalts can change without any such preservation of a 'single unique entity', as with Woodruff Smith's own example, of a 'modern sculpture' which turned out to be a fountain. The reliance upon the real continuum from which two gestalts were drawn is preserved, but no secure 'object'. Why? Woodruff Smith forgot the spray of the fountain – how much of the spray was in his first 'object', the modern sculpture, and how much was not? Manifestly, two quite different 'objects' were selected, as they always are. The reality of nature is proved at the same time as the unreliability of our current objectifications. To quote Alexander Bryan Johnson – and we should all be rereading him at this historical juncture – 'Language implies a oneness to which nature conforms not.'[3] The trap for the Cartesians lies in the fact that in deliberate mutuality we have *to presuppose* onenesses, our 'determinable X's', in order to communicate about nature at all. What the Cartesians do is to take their own presuppositions for gospel, and that is a real illusion.

Oxford

NOTES

1 Tony Durham, 'Software's time-bombs', *Guardian*, 23 June 1988, p. 27.
2 David Woodruff Smith, 'The case of the exploding perception', *Synthese*, 41 (1979), pp. 239–69.
3 Alexander Bryan Johnson, *A Treatise on Language*, ed. David Rynin (New York: Dover Publications, 1968).

ELIZABETH WRIGHT

- Peter Brooker, *Bertolt Brecht: Dialectics, Poetry, Politics* (London: Croom Helm, 1988), 259 pp., £30.00

What is the current status of Brecht as a political writer? In the GDR Brecht no longer holds his one-time prime position. In the FRG he is regarded as a pedagogue of the theatre, who oversimplifies reality. A still-prevailing view, only occasionally challenged, is to see Brecht as moving through three phases, from an early subjectivist phase to a mid-period rationalist to a supposed dialectical compromise of the problems of phase one and two in a late 'mature' phase.

Integral to the theory of the three phases is the idea of ultimate continuity. What is seen as the turning-point in Brecht's development, his encounter with Marxism in the mid-1920s and his subsequent transition from a supposed subjectivist phase into an objectivist one, is seen as a crude dialectical move, read differently by East and West. The East sees the three-phase syndrome as a developing Marxist aesthetic, moving from anarchism to a crude form of communism to a Marxist-humanist classic. The West reads it as an outcome of Brecht's personal psychology, seeing the young Brecht as floundering in an anarchistic phase, subsequently 'disciplined' by Marxism, finally seeing the humanist light in the 'great' plays. This led to a tendency to split Brecht the Marxist thinker from Brecht the 'intuitive' poet. In both Germanys this view has been challenged by up-and-coming scholars and playwrights (some playwrights, like Peter Handke, repudiate him; others, like Heiner Müller, 'refunction' him, using his work as 'material' in Brecht's own sense), but in Britain critics continue to turn out canonized readings and producers orthodox productions.

Peter Brooker's book is therefore all the more timely and welcome, since it sets out to refute that view of Brecht which situates him at any time as either a propagandist, a camp-follower of the bourgeois aesthetic, or as a compromiser between the two. His declared aim is rather to reclaim him as 'the outstanding representative this century of an attempt to politicise art and culture from an informed Marxist perspective', in the face of 'self-protective or encorporative readings from Marxist and bourgeois humanist criticism alike' (p. 4).

Brooker presents Brecht as a dialectical materialist from the very beginning, prising his concepts away from bourgeois aesthetics. He argues forcibly that epic theatre and its related concepts of *gestus* and *Verfremdungseffekt* were dialectical devices from the very start, in that *gestus* both interrupts and reveals, and *Verfremdung*, far from merely being a formalistic device encouraging 'fresh seeing', negates the self-evident in order to transform it as the 'newly intelligible', thereby repositioning the spectator in ideology and history (p. 83). Brooker extrapolates a broad definition of dialectical materialism as 'committed to the idea of change, including the revision of its own form, and this, says Lenin, is a mark of its comprehensiveness and richness compared with the common idea of evolution' (p. 29). Brooker's book is an historical demonstration that Brecht, in developing his political aesthetic, drew upon dialectical materialism throughout his work, whether poetry, drama, or critical commentaries. Brooker relates the developments he sees in Brecht's thinking to his changing situation as a Marxist artist, admitting that Brecht's beliefs were ambiguous in that he was forced to hover between an evolutionary socialist construction and a dialectical continuum, necessitating a Marxist theatre which both demonstrated and produced dialectical materialism, with 'Brecht the materialist and Brecht the dialectician pulled as it were in opposite directions' (p. 213).

In arguing his case, Brooker does not engage in a textual reading of Brecht. He relies mainly on source material, some of it being Brecht's poetry and drama, but the bulk of it either his critical writings or the writings of his fellow-Marxists. The investigation is therefore pitched at a 'factual' historical level, with the scare quotes round the factual taken for granted. That is to say, Brooker says from the outset that there are many Brechts and this is his reading, but then relies heavily on what Brecht and others actually say. Thus this is an investigation of the artist as a man rather than the artist as a text. Although at one point Brooker asserts he does not wish to suggest that 'Brecht saw himself sole authority over the meaning of his texts, or that there is no contradiction between his theory and practice' (p. 187), his study does come across as a positivist enterprise, without being fully declared as such. Brecht and others are taken at their word, and these words are full of meaning. Nevertheless, this method, if at times a little wearying in its unacknowledged intentionalism, has the virtue of meeting the establishment critics of Brecht the man and his work on their own ground, something that has not been attempted before. For that reason alone, even if it were not for the wealth of useful information and sound analysis, this study is a landmark in English Brecht criticism.

Girton College, Cambridge

DAVID AMIGONI

- Robert Sullivan, *Christopher Caudwell* (London: Croom Helm, 1988), 208 pp., £27.50

In what sense does Christopher Caudwell figure as a twentieth-century critic? All of the major critical works that were published under this name – *Illusion and Reality*, the *Studies* and *Further Studies in a Dying Culture* and *Romance and Realism* – appeared after the 29-year-old Christopher St John Sprigg had been killed fighting fascism in Spain. Though committed to the elaboration of a Marxist theory of the social function of literature, the *œuvre* has not been wholeheartedly embraced by current twentieth-century Marxist critics. Terry Eagleton's *Criticism and Ideology* (1976), an attempt to swing British Marxism into theoretical line with Europe, could only see English insularity in the work of Caudwell, plus an alarming tendency to mount 'hectic forays into and out of alien [disciplinary] territories'. However, if Eagleton's period of Althusserian commitment signalled the expulsion of Caudwell's work from the Marxist canon, the counter-reaction to Althusser displayed an eagerness to engage with it anew; in *Marxism and Literature* (1977) Raymond Williams suggested that the interrogatory approach to 'orthodox' Marxist positions that his book attempted to advance enabled him to reread Caudwell's aesthetics with new eyes – though he never specified the nature of the vision. Edward Thompson's essay of the same year did, however, offer a concrete rereading of Caudwell's project, which jettisoned certain parts of the *œuvre* – notably *Illusion and Reality* – in order to highlight the aspect of ideological critique at work in the texts. Robert Sullivan's new book on Caudwell for the series 'Critics of the Twentieth Century' proposes to continue the process of rereading and reassessment.

Sullivan's lucid and original study claims that a rereading of Caudwell is called for because, since the mid-1970s, the critical problematic has been radically restructured; Caudwell's work, once denigrated, now answers many of the questions that the problematic poses. Thus, with the category of the subject having moved to the centre of theoretical debate, Caudwell's concern with the social construction of the psyche and the human individual needs fresh consideration. Similarly, with the sign being seen less as a component in an abstract, self-regulating and self-referential system, and more as a discursive and inter-subjective generator of meaning, Caudwell's observations on the communication process assume a new relevance. Finally, in the light of Fredric Jameson's recent attempt to theorize the effect of the socially symbolic act of narration upon the collective political unconscious, Caudwell's concern to explain the transformative function that poetry (illusion) performs upon structures of social organization (reality) — essentially the purpose of *Illusion and Reality* — can be seen as a parallel enterprise. The parallel extends to the ambitious intellectual embrace attempted by each project. Jameson's attempt to synthesize Hegelian Marxism, Althusserianism and psycho-analysis is matched by Caudwell, who negotiated the disciplines of biology, psychology, anthropology, linguistics, and literary criticism, and sought to synthesize them through the master discipline of Marxism. In the face of this eclecticism, Sullivan modestly admits that he has not found it possible to follow his subject's intricate line of thought at every turn. Even so, Sullivan does promise to elucidate 'the genesis of [the] discourses' that come together to produce texts such as *Illusion and Reality*, and thus to show Caudwell as 'a subject . . . reacting to the object of his own historical time'; this, however, is a commitment which is not wholly fulfilled, for it stands in a relationship of tension to Sullivan's determination to 'prove' Caudwell's relevance to the present, to make him a twentieth-century critic after our own hearts.

Sullivan begins by dealing with the poetry, technical writing and popular crime novels that appeared under the name of Christopher St John Sprigg, and though he traces intellectual common ground between these and the later criticism, he sees this material as a counterpoint to the politically engaged nature of the later work, which appeared under the name of Christopher Caudwell, 'cultural anatomist'. The change of name was indicative of a change of community — Caudwell left the world of middle-class small business and journalism and joined the Communist Party, serving the Poplar branch in London's East End — and a change of world view. And it is a discussion of the change of world view manifest in *Illusion and Reality* that constitutes the centre of Sullivan's study and the originality of his perspective.

Illusion and Reality is a difficult text to untie. It is an uneasy attempt to synthesize a constellation of disparate disciplinary perspectives. It begins as an anthropological discourse upon the function of the symbolic in primitive patterns of social organization, and the different roles performed by 'scientific' and 'imaginative' signs in advanced societies. It goes on to offer a narrative account of the history of English poetry, or the history of the imaginative symbol in patterns of English class relations. This diachronic perspective seeks further verification through a synchronic engagement with a range of natural and social scientific discourses; principally discourses on the biological and psychological nature of the human subject, which wrestle with the problem of the capacity of the subject for social adaptation. The problem of adaptation is to be resolved by identifying the precise nature of the interactive relationship between structures of mental fantasy (illusion) and the social and material environment (reality); the proposed resolution being negotiated via an explicit set of arguments directed against asocial Freudian accounts of the interiorized nature of fantasies or dreams. These various discursive strands are woven together into a thesis that projects the ultimate resolution through the identification of the 'sources of poetry'. *Illusion and Reality* is a hard text from which to extract an uncontestable definition, but poetry stands as a mode of symbolic utterance which, by dint of a 'social ego', or a collective identity formed by an inter-subjective network of signs, places the subject in an active imaginative relationship to a constantly changing social environment and patterns of social relations. Clearly *Illusion and Reality* moves through a more complex weave of positions than the relatively straightforward ideological critique offered by *Studies in a Dying Culture*.

Sullivan's originality lies in his reading and rehabilitation of *Illusion and Reality* which challenges Edward Thompson's disparaging judgement on the text. Thompson was of the opinion that if Caudwell's reputation as a critic were to be salvaged at all, then it would have to be at the price of 'downgrading' the difficult and contradictory *Illusion and Reality*; an act that would allow the later and more coherent *Studies in a Dying Culture* to shine through and display Caudwell as a critic of note. Against this, Sullivan defends *Illusion and Reality*. He does so by arguing that it was the *Studies* which had a detrimental effect on *Illusion and Reality*; rather than being written later than *Illusion*, the *Studies* were being written simultaneously, and their separate insights were channelled into a project that had a potential coherence all of its own. The result was an unbalanced *Illusion and Reality*. Sullivan reaches this conclusion via an examination of early drafts of *Illusion and Reality*, and he uses the fruits of this research to come at Caudwell from a different angle. In effect, he is arguing that Caudwell had elaborated a theory of symbolic action and its complex dialectical relationship to social and material reality *before* his wholehearted embrace of Marxism; and this amounts to the difference between on the one hand looking at Caudwell as a critic completed by Marxism (essentially Thompson's perspective), and on the other seeing Marxism as something more contingent to his critical project, which is the perspective that Sullivan implicitly develops. This assists Sullivan's broader aim, which is to liberate Caudwell from debates generated exclusively within the discipline of Marxism and thereby implicate him in a set of literary critical debates that speak to us now.

Sullivan's approach here is to be broadly welcomed; if new readers are going to be drawn to Caudwell, there will have to be something in it for them. Even so, his chapter 'Implicating Caudwell' suggests that the welcome should be extended tentatively. Sullivan is perhaps too inclined to look for 'something very Caudwellian' in Frye, Lacan, Jameson, and Volosinov. Certainly, there are significant points of contact, but there are also notable differences, principally due to the fact that each critic – although a twentieth-century critic – is situated in a different historical and cultural space, negotiating a different set of discourses and institutions, and thereby implicated in a different rhetorical situation. In essence, though Sullivan claims to explain the 'genesis of discourses' comprising Caudwell's work, what his study lacks is a sustained attempt to theorize the contestatory historical relationships between the various strands of critical discourse that Caudwell was negotiating and Sullivan is tracing. For Sullivan adopts something like an empiricist's balance-sheet account of the process of intellectual production; Caudwell is consistently found to be owing to one source, and in the debt of another. This promotes a curiously non-discursive approach to the question of the genesis of Caudwellian discourse, which is manifest in Sullivan's critical understanding of the function of rhetoric. Sullivan tellingly sees the Marxian vocabulary at work in *Illusion and Reality* as 'rhetorical' in the sense that it merely embellishes an intention that pre-exists its deployment, and this means that he fails to engage with Caudwell's Marxism as a form of rhetoric that contests, re-shapes, and negotiates the *other* forms of rhetoric that are brought together in *Illusion and Reality*. For it is precisely the clashes between these contestatory forms of rhetoric – the dialogical tensions that are created by an attempt to synthesize the knowledges of Marxism, psychoanalysis, anthropology and linguistics – that fuel and drive the controversies within the various knowledge communities (and here I am assuming that Marxism itself is a heterogeneous knowledge community) which have sought to possess, appropriate and contest Caudwell's project. Such an historicized under-standing of rhetoric seems to me to be a fundamental condition of the possibility of rereading Caudwell's status as a twentieth-century critic, for it accounts for the historically specific discursive dialogues that have had, and continue to have, the effect of keeping the texts 'open' to new readings in new contexts.

At one point, Robert Sullivan refers to Jameson's *The Political Unconscious* as a 'juggling act'. This metaphor comes close to a conception of that text explored by Dominic La Capra in *Re-thinking Intellectual History* (1983), a collection which does much to theorize a dialogical approach to the reading of the artefacts of intellectual history. It would have been appropriate for Sullivan to consider more searchingly the dialogical juggling act performed by discourses at play in the critical works of Christopher Caudwell.

Liverpool Polytechnic

WILLY MALEY

- David Cairns and Shaun Richards, *Writing Ireland: Colonialism, Nationalism and Culture* (Manchester: Manchester University Press, 1988), 178 pp., £21.50 (hardback), £5.95 (paperback)

The cultural construction of the Irish as a people placed 'beyond the pale' of an assumed English civility is one of the earliest and most enduring myths manufactured by the English press. It is a prejudice with an exceptionally long pedigree and a very complicated history. The traditional opposition of English culture and Irish anarchy is so pervasive that it not only saturates the texts of certain dominant minorities, but invades those discourses which set out to undermine it. One recent example of this unwitting repetition of the colonial move arises in *Writing Ireland: Colonialism, Nationalism and Culture*, a text whose authors, David Cairns and Shaun Richards, are quite clearly committed to opposing the entrenched colonialism of the English relationship with Ireland. They open their study of literature and identity in nineteenth- and twentieth-century Ireland with a chapter entitled 'What ish my nation?', an historical introduction advertised as 'an outline of the originary moment of the colonial relationship and its aftermath'. This theoretical preoccupation with origins and aftermaths is, I shall argue, quite in keeping with English colonial practice.

Where to begin? Cairns and Richards begin by quoting Edward Said: 'Beginnings have to be made for each project in such a way as to enable what follows from them' (p. 1). They then proceed with the 'necessary prelude' to their survey of literature and identity in modern Ireland,

> an outline of the originary moment of the colonial relationship and its aftermath; consequently, our examination of the cultural engagements of the English and Irish peoples begins in the sixteenth century at a crucial moment for English State and cultural formation.

This 'consequently' has some important consequences for the kind of criticism Cairns and Richards engage in. Their claim to be offering an outline of 'the originary moment of the colonial relationship' between England and Ireland does not quite square with our knowledge of history. If we were to commence a critique of the English colonial subjection of Ireland with the evocation of an 'originary moment' in that relationship, it would be historically incorrect to take the sixteenth century as such 'an originary moment'. The most 'uncultured' of natives knows that the originary moment occurred four centuries earlier. We 'cultured' readers, sensitive to literary allusion, might say that one who professes to locate the beginning of the English colonial connection with Ireland in the sixteenth century 'thrusteth even into the middest', and inadvertently follows in the footsteps of the colonizer. Cairns and Richards are eager to ground their criticism in 'history': 'Our beginning lies with the reality of the historic relationship of Ireland with England; a relationship of the colonized and the colonizer.' My beginning also draws upon history as a way of approaching the altercations, alternations, and alterations of literature and identity in Ireland, but from a different angle. To follow the contours of conflict, crisis, and change in Renaissance Ireland, one has to be particularly attentive to historical difference, as well as literary allusion. I do not consider the sixteenth century to be an 'originary moment' in the colonial relationship between England and Ireland. A turning-point, certainly, and a predictable point of departure for modern critics, but not an originary moment, not the starting-point of the Anglo-Irish colonial relationship. Ireland's cultural memory is rather more elephantine than that of most of its professional critics. Where the authors of *Writing Ireland* conjure up the sixteenth century in order to begin their assessment of literature and identity in modern Ireland, this writer goes back to medieval history as a 'necessary prelude' to the study of English culture in early modern Ireland.

D. B. Quinn has posited Ireland as

> a unique example of a territory which was colonised in the twelfth and thirteenth centuries in a feudal setting and was recolonised in the sixteenth and seventeenth centuries in a post-feudal setting. It has, strongly marked, a 'native' problem, and it has, at several levels, the problem of a settler community – of the 'Old English' of the medieval settlement in relation to the 'New English' of the early modern settlement, and of both in relation to the metropolitan government in England.[1]

It is the 'several levels' of the settler problem which make early modern Ireland a particularly intractable text for historians, and, I would argue, it is exactly the tensions between competing colonial communities which work their way through the writings of Spenser and his associates in New English literary circles.[2] For now our concern is with the roots of the 'Old English' estrangement from the central authorities, an estrangement whose origins go back to the first institution of English power in Ireland, and to a time when the Old English were themselves newcomers. My contention is that the 'originary moment' of English colonialism and the source of colonial nationalism are coincidental.

Giraldus Cambrensis is, famously, the architect of English anti-Irish prejudice. His two books on the subjection of England's primary colonial possession were reproduced with depressing regularity during the formative years of the Tudor recolonization. The first of these, *The Topography of Ireland*, he originally delivered as a series of Latin lectures at the University of Oxford around 1187, almost exactly eight centuries ago. By his own account, these seminars were a resounding success, and contributed to the stimulation of consumer demand for the series of manuscripts subsequently thrown into circulation. Ireland was clearly a highly marketable literary commodity long before its exploitation as an English dependency, and before the incidence of any sixteenth-century originary moment. 'Ireland' has always been taken literally, as a *littoral* tabula rasa. Indeed, the cultural capital to be extracted from Ireland has, from the very outset, acted as a stimulus to English colonizers on a par with any 'purely' economic advantages. The second work undertaken by Cambrensis, *Expugnatio Hibernica*, or *The Conquest of Ireland*, appeared in print and in English translation for the second edition of Holinshed's *Chronicles*, published in 1587. Holinshed, who had sojourned briefly in Ireland a decade earlier, provided Elizabethan culture with a wealth of misinformation about Ireland and the Irish which was easily assimilated by renaissance poets and playwrights such as Spenser and Shakespeare. Thus the advent of print accelerated considerably that process of textual colonization inaugurated by a medieval professor in the pay of a pocket of disenfranchised English aristocrats. The successful seminars of this innovative ideologue constitute one of the originary moments in English colonial history.[3]

Spurred on by the success of his *Topography*, and 'at the insistent request of many men of rank', Giraldus set to work sometime around 1188–9 on the *Conquest*. If his literary debut had been a description of 'the events and scenes of time past', then its follow-up, the *Conquest*, would address 'contemporary events'.[4] In the *Conquest*, Giraldus delineates divisions within the settler community, and between that community and the English crown. In foregrounding the political differences between court and colony, he cites a speech by Maurice Fitzgerald, a leading member of the newly established colonial elite, to illustrate the predicament of the vanguard of the adventuring class:

> Whie then doo we tarie? And wherefore doo we so linger? Is there anie hope of releefe from home? No no, the matter is otherwise, and we in woorse case. For as we be odious and hatefull to the Irishmen, even so we now are reputed: for Irishmen are become hatefull to our owne nation and countrie, and so are we odious both to the one and the other.[5]

The questions of identity posed by Maurice turn not on some simplistic English–Irish opposition, but, more problematically, revolve around the pronounced cultural confusion of an intermediate social grouping with firm anchorage in neither neighbour nation. Here, in 'history', we find none of the stultifying dualism, the stupefying metaphysics, of certain forms of literary theory.

In Shakespeare's Macmorris, we see a similar interrogation of easy assumptions of national identity. We know that Shakespeare leaned heavily on Holinshed for the history plays of the 1580s and 1590s. One would expect him to rely therefore on the Irish section of that work for his references to 'Irish' character. I am not the first to link Macmorris with the Old English, but as far as I know I am the first to suggest Holinshed as the source of this character, and to further imply that the origins of this identity crisis, this apparently modern questioning of cultural identity, lie in the twelfth century.[6] 'New' critics have readily followed the false lead given by Philip Edwards in *Threshold of a Nation*, and have, accordingly, been carried over the threshold of historic reality and into embarrassingly ahistorical and anglocentric positions.[7] Macmorris is almost certainly a Palesman. Macmorris, or 'son of Morris', belongs to a clan which traces its ancestry back to the so-called 'Anglo-Norman' conquest. John Gillingham has recently challenged the traditional use of the term 'Anglo-Norman' to designate the first settlers in Ireland. He is convinced that the anodyne reconstitution of the twelfth-century *English* colonization as an 'Anglo-Norman' affair is a piece of modern historical revision which plays down the significance of English colonialism in the medieval period, either for political ends, or through an obsession with looking to the Elizabethan era, or to a Renaissance which closely resembles the Elizabethan era, for the origins of everything. In Gillingham's view,

> those who point to the sixteenth century as the starting point of it all are just a little bit wide of the mark – roughly 400 years wide of the mark. The formative experience was not the forward policy adopted by the Elizabethans in the late 1560s, but the forward policy adopted by Henry II in the early 1170s. This is crucially important because it means that these imperialist attitudes are much more deeply ingrained than people realise.[8]

This modern critical tendency to treat English colonialism as an early modern development rather than a medieval departure, Gillingham attributes in part to the 'myth of the Renaissance', one of the sustaining fictions of English culture, which automatically degrades the political achievements, administrative innovations and textual remains of English society in the middle ages. It is as though all the New English publicity produced by Spenser and company has become institutionalized; their claims to be the harbingers of an improved civility now taken for granted; their literary productions canonized; their protestations of national pre-eminence unchallenged, and their professions of cultural superiority unquestioned.

One can see the attraction of beginning in the sixteenth century, and of beginning with Shakespeare. An established Elizabethan text offers a convenient way of *staging history*. One can see the logic of looking to the sixteenth century for early 'evidence' of colonial discourse. The surviving documentation for the period is more easily accessible than that of preceding ages. The availability of printed sources and an ideology of cultural progress have ensured that what historians refer to as the early modern period, and literary critics prefer to call the Renaissance, takes precedence over a supposedly obscure, alien and regressive medieval epoch.[9] One can see, too, why nineteenth-century nationalist historians would have wanted, strategically, to site the 'originary moment' of English colonialism in the sixteenth century. That way the rightful heirs of the Old English would be exonerated from their part in the English colonial drama, and given dispensation on grounds of religious identity and nationalist rhetoric. One can see how this comfortable little conspiracy of silence on the long history of English interference in Ireland has met the needs of the modern inheritors of both English traditions, Old and New alike. The professional nationalist historian would have us believe that the origins of English colonialism are to be found in the protestant reformation and, in Spenser's words, 'Newe Englishe mens intruding'.[10] The English critic sees no farther than the printed sources, and accepts the sixteenth-century recolonization as a first footing, reading the Elizabethan reconquest as an 'originary moment'. This process of tailoring history to suit one's own political perspective is understandable. No critic can convincingly claim neutrality with regard to a text as difficult as 'Ireland' is. Reading the Irish question historically is an extremely demanding task. That 'Lethargie' which Spenser suggested as the probable cause of the Old English propensity to 'quite forget their Countrey and their owne names' remains an obstacle in the path of a radical demythification of the English colonial legacy.[11]

The question of Shakespeare's Macmorris, the question of *cultural* identity, which Cairns and Richards, in keeping with a recent trend in new English criticism, have confined to a banal instance of *national* difference, as though Shakespeare were simply reflecting some contemporary English disdain for 'the Irish', is one of supreme urgency, requiring a criticism that goes beyond the meta-nationalist, cosmopolitan concourse of Joyce *et al*. By now, it is hoped, the difficulty of the Irish text, and the impossibility of reading early modern Ireland in terms of a straight forward struggle between some self-evident English culture and an untouched Gaelic civilization, is understood. Post-colonialism, to which the glossy cover of *Writing Ireland* refers, is a word with no history in an Irish context. Or, rather, it is a word with an all too obvious history – as the last refuge of a select coterie of Old English authors. The James Deanes and the James Heaneys who occupy the bulk of this book are the modern representatives of Macmorrisism. Who talks of my Nation? By class and culture these latter-day professors of *politesse* are palesmen, seonins, little more than guardians of an *alternative* tradition in English culture.

Traditionally, struggles within, over, and between English, old and new, have assumed a colonial character. It is this inter-English dispute, this play-off between cultured elites in a colonial context, which I find most fascinating. No literary critic has hitherto considered the question of 'English' Renaissance self-fashioning, or role-playing, in an Irish setting, although Brendan Bradshaw and Nicholas Canny, two prominent and prolific Irish historians, have published case studies of such personal promotion for, respectively, a Gaelic Irish chieftain and a New English earl.[12] English Renaissance studies has much to learn from historians of early modern Ireland, who invariably deal in a much more material way with the consequences of the 'spread of English'.

'What ish my nation?' is certainly a question prompted by the crisis of identity precipitated upon both colonized and colonizer by the inexorable surge of modern capitalism. It is important to differentiate, though, between the rank rhetoric of the newcomers and the real resistance of the natives. The undecidability at the heart of Irish nationalism, the mystical shell of its violent dialectic, derives from the historical position of the Old English, that intermediary colonial class which governed the English pale for the first half of the eight centuries of English interference in Ireland. The spectre of Old English conservatism, albeit subversive at times, still haunts Irish nationalism. The mercenary Macmorris, muddled in the field, represents not the archetypal stage Irishman the authors of *Writing Ireland* would have us see him as, but the vacillating palesman, deracinated, uprooted, astray in the no-man's-land of opportunism, defeatism, and professional chicanery. The question is purely academic, staged, rhetorical, put solely for dramatic effect. The meta-nationalism of Macmorris is not a question, never mind a problem. It is a pose, a posture of puzzlement assumed by early modernists, modernists and post-modernists alike, and one which stands between us and a thorough knowledge of the national question.

Writing Ireland is a book which demands to be read by all those interested in literary theory, colonial history, and the deregulation, devolution or disintegration of 'English'. If, however, 'the end of English' is to entail more than the transfer of power from one colonial class to another, then critics will have to take native wit, and native power, into account, particularly if they decide to engage with history in the course of their literary endeavours.[13] If we accept the thesis that 'All the abominations of the English have their origin in the Irish Pale' (Engels to Marx, 24 October 1869), our commitment to the de(con)struction, or decolonization, of English culture ought to begin with a thorough review of its Irish stage, which goes beyond the customary patronizing and pat references to the so-called 'stage-Irish'. The act of staging, or paging, history performs no progressive function. To constitute a really radical textual practice, the process of writing Ireland has to ra(n)ge beyond the page of accepted English literary history. This, the book of the same name, with its limited questions and contexts, singularly fails to do.

University of Strathclyde

NOTES

1 David Beers Quinn, 'Ireland and sixteenth century European expansion', *Historical Studies*, I (1958), p. 20.
2 For an account of the Elizabethan stage of this process of alienation, see Ciaran Brady, 'Conservative subversives: the community of the Pale and the Dublin administration, 1556–86', *Historical Studies*, XV (1985), pp. 11–32.

3 Evidence for Holinshed's presence in Ireland is to be found in William Pinkerton, 'Barnaby Googe', *Notes and Queries*, III (1863), p. 182. For a conjectural essay on Shakespeare and Ireland, see W. J. Lawrence, 'Was Shakespeare ever in Ireland?', *Shakespeare Jahrbuch*, XLII (1906), pp. 65–75.

4 See Giraldus Cambrensis, *Expugnatio Hibernica: The Conquest of Ireland*, edited with translation and notes by A. B. Scott and F. X. Martin (Dublin: Royal Irish Academy, 1978), especially pp. 267–84, 'Giraldus as historian'.

5 *Holinshed's Chronicles of England, Scotland and Ireland*, vol. VI, *Ireland* (London: 1808), p. 152.

6 See J. O. Bartley, *Teague, Shenkin and Sawney* (Cork: Cork University Press, 1954), pp. 16–17; Sir D. Plunkett Barton, *Links between Ireland and Shakespeare* (Dublin and London: 1919), pp. 114–36; W. J. Lawrence, op. cit., p. 70; Edward D. Snyder, 'The wild Irish: a study of some English satires against the Irish, Scots, and Welsh', *Modern Philology*, XVII, 12 (1920), pp. 147–85. For an entertaining, if theoretically lax, polemic on the subject, see John Arden, 'Rug-headed Irish kerns and British poets', *New Statesman*, 13 July 1979, pp. 56–7.

7 Philip Edwards, *Threshold of a Nation* (Cambridge: Cambridge University Press, 1979), pp. 75–8. Edwards seems to be the source of the myth of the 'Irish' captain in Essex's army, repeated by Gary Taylor in the 1982 Oxford edition of *Henry V*. In a footnote to his 'Conservative subversives', Ciaran Brady refers to an Old English treatise which is most likely behind this case of mistaken identity: 'A discourse [on] ... the planting of colonies' (1598) (PRO, SP 63/102 pt 4/75); the author further argues, 'the extract of the English nation there [in Ireland] ought not to be excepted unto but rather employed against the Irish' and complains that 'the descent of the English, to their great grief are here [in England] called and counted Irish though they are reputed and called English' (p. 32, n. 46). Essex's Irish captain was probably an Oxford-educated Old English lawyer. Among those taken in by the myth are Stephen Greenblatt, 'Invisible bullets: Renaissance authority and its subversion, *Henry IV* and *Henry V*', in Jonathan Dollimore and Alan Sinfield (eds), *Political Shakespeare: New Essays in Cultural Materialism* (Manchester: Manchester University Press, 1985), p. 42, and Dollimore and Sinfield themselves, 'History and ideology: the instance of *Henry V*', in J. Drakakis (ed.), *Alternative Shakespeares* (London: Methuen, 1985), p. 224.

8 John Gillingham, 'Images of Ireland 1170–1600: the origins of English imperialism', *History Today*, 37 (1987), p. 17.

9 For a radical reappraisal of Renaissance humanism, see Anthony Grafton and Lisa Jardine, *From Humanism to the Humanities: Education and the Liberal Arts in Fifteenth- and Sixteenth-Century Europe* (Cambridge, Mass.: Harvard University Press, 1986). The introduction, pp. xi–xvi, questions the traditional humanist assumptions concerning the progressive character of humanism. An informed latter-day Old English view of the subject is put forward by Katherine Walsh, 'The Reformation and education – humanist theory and sectarian practice', *Studies* (Autumn 1975), pp. 215–29.

10 Edmund Spenser, *A View of the Present State of Ireland*, ed. W. L. Renwick (London: Scholartis Press, 1934), p. 195.

11 ibid., p. 84.

12 Brendan Bradshaw, 'Manus "the Magnificent": O'Donnell as Renaissance prince', in A. Cosgrove and D. McCartney (eds), *Studies in Irish History* (Dublin: 1979); Nicholas Canny, *The Upstart Earl: a Study of the Social and*

Mental World of Richard Boyle, First Earl of Cork, 1566–1643 (Cambridge: Cambridge University Press, 1982).

13 For a rear-view of this all-too-familiar mid-life 'crisis', this New English version of the male menopause, see Terry Eagleton, 'The end of English', *Textual Practice*, 1, 1 (Spring 1987), pp. 1–9. A more serious and scholarly survey of the break-up of English is Colin MacCabe, 'Broken English', *Critical Quarterly*, 28, 1 & 2 (1986), pp. 3–14.

IAN WHITEHOUSE

• Paul Carter, *The Road to Botany Bay* (London: Faber & Faber, 1987), 384 pp., £14.95

• Krim Benterrak, Stephen Muecke, and Paddy Roe, *Reading the Country* (Fremantle, Western Australia: Fremantle Art Centre Press, 1984), 243 pp., A$29.95

• Robert Sandford and Mel Buschert, *Panoramas of the Canadian Rockies* (Banff, Alberta: Summerthought Publications, 1987), 104 pp., C$20

These three books, each in its own very different way, gaze toward that horizon of past events in which frontiers were established, lands named, explored, mapped, and occupied, and 'histories' initiated. Each describes the process by which a particular space of cultural history was constructed. All three deal with the colonization of a specific place, the first two with Australia, the third with the Canadian Rockies. Paradoxically, while each offers to our readerly attention the material actuality of place and history, of maps and photographs, of accounts, log books, and reports, they do so only to shift that attention onto the gaze which initially produced the artefacts and their consequent histories. It is the roads, the railways, the nomadic routes by which the land is traversed and occupied which are of interest to the individual writers. It is how the place is seen, rather than the scenic, which occupies their attention. However, in the assumptions which govern their own individual gaze a marked difference arises. Indeed, the coordinates provided by these three viewpoints constitute a critical compass which allows us to explore that place of colonization, that space in which (hi)stories are constructed in the very process of naming and mapping, reading and reporting, tracing and tracking.

Panoramas of the Canadian Rockies ostensibly presents itself as a celebration of the 'grandeur' of one of North America's largest mountain ranges. Impressively adorned with photographs of consummate skill and artistry, this book of image and essay is of the kind which, in North America, finds its way on to a bookshelf as a memento of one of those 'unforgettable experiences of our encounter with nature'. Indeed, with its utilization of the latest optical technology involving format cameras with rotating lenses capable of encompassing 360 degrees, any urban tourist nostalgic for the 'wilderness' can simply open the book to any one of a number of eye-catching fold-outs and immediately be encircled by an scene of persuasive beauty. Few professional photographers possess the acumen evidenced by the collection of images constructed by Mel Buschert's photographic eye. The 'panorama', the all encompassing view, the invitation to master immensity itself is all there, simply waiting for the reading subject.

If the book went no further than this, however, while it might very well merit attention in a photographer's year-book or a climber's guide to as yet unscaled peaks, it would hardly be the subject matter for critical inquiry. And so the question must be asked as to why such a book deserves a larger reading audience than simply that defined by the 'experience of being there'. To answer that question is to return again to the idea of the gaze and to what the eye actually sees, that is, to the image which is constructed and presented to the reading subject. It is at this point that the idea of 'panorama' comes to the foreground, along with a 'tourist' who sees it, and the image-maker who provides the lens through which that which is seen becomes naturalized, that is, *scenic*. In addition to the photographic realism of a panorama, a universal view, of the Rockies, the book offers a series of *essays*, personal views of a more limited nature, by Robert Sandford, a 'specialist in landscape and cultural interpretation'. Sandford's essays review the history of the Canadian Pacific Railroads's encounter with the Rocky Mountains and of the subsequent construction of luxury hotels adjacent to the most 'scenic' areas along its lines. What Sandford's eye allows us to see is precisely the covert relationship between money, leisure, and 'grandeur'. It is his astute observation that it was not until people could travel through the Rockies in leisured comfort and safety that 'these mountains assumed a grandeur worthy of celebration'. Sandford also opens a vista in which the creation of a climber's and adventurer's paradise follows upon the circulation of stories and photographs concerning unnamed and unclimbed peaks which rose 'in every direction from the spectacular rail line that pierced the very centre of the Rockies'. Thus, fantasy and photography merge in the profitable enterprise of a 'wilderness ready to be conquered'. This imaginative space was quickly colonized by tourists from all over the world. In each of these scenic places, in the midst of what had hitherto been uninhabited wilderness, suddenly a settlement sprang up. To bring that reality into sharp relief, Sandford cites a railroad worker's description of one of the 'colonies' located at the Banff Springs Hotel in 1925:

> The truth is that I could not take beautiful Banff seriously. I dreamed it, and like so many dreams it was at once absurd and beautiful. On a pine-covered bank . . . above the crystal foam of the Bow I came to a giant castle. It had no business being there, for when I was thereabouts so long ago, no one could have thought of it. The dream castle was full . . . of people who talked all at once and I saw in a moment that they were not real. If any of us workers of the old days had seen their likes we should have thought we had delirium tremens. (pp. 14)

The sight of rich, leisured members of a privileged class no longer causes delirium to old timers of the area. As Sandford ironically reflects, 'for decades a photograph of the lake and the valley . . . has graced the back of the Canadian twenty dollar bill, a subtle reminder, perhaps, of the extent to which tourism in the Rockies contributes to the national economy'. Sandford's own narrative economy, itself rich in the celebration of the individual spirit, contributes generously to our understanding of the ways in which panoramas are created, naturalized, and inhabited.

Reading the Country, on the other hand, immediately sets out to displace such cognitive frames as the Individual, Freedom, and Authority, along with the social ideologies which privilege these categories. Rather than constructing a story of the romantic individual's fight against an unforgiving nature, the book attempts to construct a theory of place, 'a method of charting the meaning of those specific places in which people must find a way to live in one manner or another' (pp. 12). To construct such a theory is to put into question the very notions of 'reading', 'seeing', and the 'essential nature of things'. This in turn necessitates an awareness of the historical and cultural specificities which allow a people, a collective, to make sense of things, that is, to 'see' and to 'read'.

In *Reading the Country*, then, the ethos of the individual gives way to a politics of place, a poetics of difference. The specific place in question is an area in north-west Australia, Roebuck Plains. The book itself marries three distinct 'readings' of the Plains. The first is a narrative and photographic account provided by Stephen Muecke, lecturer, writer, white native son. The second reading, in the form of paintings, comes from Krim Benterrak, a Morroccan-born immigrant to Australia. The third reading is spoken through the voice of Paddy Roe – a Nyiginal, an Aborigine born on the Plains – and takes the form of songs, stories, and memories transcribed by Muecke While these three readings cover diverse cultural and historical fields, the aim is not to enclose the country, but to traverse it, to show how the traces, left by tracking, both make the country and are made by it. As opposed to a panorama, an all-encompassing view, this book offers a nomadology, a way of re-presenting in discontinuous fragments a being in place, a book with no ultimate authority or authoritative view, only an aesthetic/political stance which seeks to create a space in which singularities can be recognized and questions asked. In *Reading the Country* one recognizes familiar tracks: Deleuze, Guattari, Foucault, Barthes, Derrida, Althusser and more. Yet in this narrative space they do not appear as guarantors for some final truth or destination; rather, they act as signposts, indices for further intervention, nomadic records moving in the time and place of reading.

The Road to Botany Bay is itself intimately involved in the act of reading, or more precisely rereading. Paul Carter sets out to review the colonization of Australia by English settlers some two hundred years ago when the First Fleet sailed into Botany Bay. For much the same reasons as those set forth in Sandford's essays, Carter believes that before the country could be occupied, first it had to be created, it had to be named, mapped, imagined as an inhabitable space with horizon and history. Thus, his main focus is the reports and diaries, the log-books, maps, and comments of the first explorers and settlers, the medium of that necessary history. Unlike a traditional historical approach, however, those texts are not examined as commentaries on 'historical' events which happened and then were recorded. In Carter's rereading, the records of explorers like Cook, Flinders, Mitchell, and Stuart themselves become history, that is, history as writing. The book, subtitled 'An Essay in Spatial History', in fact charts the creation of that space called 'Australia' as it occurred in the very act of naming, in the very process of delineating and signposting. For Carter, there was not a place simply waiting to be named, but a process of naming which opened a space in which historical events were made possible.

As in *Reading the Country*, then, *The Road to Botany Bay* encourages our critical eye to attend to the ways in which traversing and describing a terrain create the possibility of a space in which 'history' can occur. The maps Carter offers for our attention, again like the nomadic records of *Reading the Country*, are incomplete, unfinished records of a journey which itself is unfinished. Like the climber's stories of unnamed peaks in Sandford's essays, these maps – over which comments are written – create a space for colonization, define an imaginary terrain in which the language of European culture can write over the (hi)stories of an Aboriginal culture. And yet the nomenclature also testifies to an uneasy fit between name and place. 'Dry River', for instance, marks an absence, a place where language no longer serves to facilitate the transition from expectation to exploitation. Instead of an imperial imposition, a kind of reciprocal determination surfaces within the space of naming and mapping, for the translation of a place-name from one continent to another does not guarantee the recreation of that place. Rather than simply importing a ready-made space inscribed in the name, the nomenclature of both Banks and Cook indicates a complex negotiation between cultural expectations and the constraints imposed by the geography itself. Thus, the naming of place takes on the character of a historical event. Similarly, the act of establishing boundaries and borders serves not only to enclose an inhabitable space, that is, a locus for scenes of domesticity, but also to open up the 'wilderness beyond' to the gaze of love and appreciation. It is Carter's attention to these covert yet complex interchanges which makes *The Road to Botany Bay* such a fascinating and important essay.

Roads and panoramas, photographs and engravings, readings and mappings – these are the topics of interest to writers who encourage us to survey the process by which the place of empire emerges. Whether read individually or collectively, *Panoramas of the Canadian Rockies*, *Reading the Country*, and *The Road to Botany Bay* will reward the critical gaze with a negotiable space for understanding the complex construction of history.

University of Wales, Cardiff

Printed in the United States
by Baker & Taylor Publisher Services